THE
ESSENTIAL WOODWORKER:
SKILLS, TOOLS AND MATERIALS

*To Violet Matilda —
a workshop widow these
many years*

THE
ESSENTIAL WOODWORKER: SKILLS, TOOLS AND MATERIALS

Robert Wearing

B. T. Batsford Ltd, London

Jacket photograph by
Tim Roberts

Figures 1 and 13 kindly supplied
by Record Tools

Photographs 2 and 3 kindly
supplied by Eclipse Tools

ISBN 0 7134 5549 7

Typeset by Speedlith Photo Litho Ltd,
Longford Trading Estate, Thomas Street,
Stretford, Manchester M32 0JT
and printed in Great Britain by
The Bath Press, Bath

for the publishers
B. T. Batsford Ltd
4 Fitzhardinge Street
London W1H 0AH

CONTENTS

INTRODUCTION

1 BASIC WOODWORKING SKILLS   8
Planing   8
Sharpening   8
Adjusting the plane   12
How to plane   15
Two planing exercises   20
Facing   21
Edging   22
Gauging   26
Producing to size   28
Squaring   28
Sawing   30
Screwing   32
Boring   33

2 MAKING A TABLE OR STOOL   35
Construction and design   35
Marking out the joints   36
Chopping mortices   41
Sawing tenons   43
Marking and chopping button
mortices   47
Planing tapers   47
Polishing insides   48
Glueing up   49
Cleaning up the outside   53
The cabinet scraper   56
Jointing the top   59
Dowelling the edge joints   61
Cleaning up the top   62
The scraper plane   63
Shaping the table top   66
Edge shaping   70
The scratch tool   71
Shrinkage buttons   75
Finishes   76
Levelling the feet   78

3 MAKING A CARCASE   79
Construction and design   79
A dowelled carcase   80
A dovetailed carcase   84

Marking and cutting dovetails   86
Marking and cutting lap dovetails   92
Shelves   94
Cabinet backs   97
The carcase glue-up   103
Door types   106
The framed door   112
   (a) grooved construction   112
   (b) rebated construction   114
Fitting a door   116
Hingeing a door   118
Fitting ball catches   120
Fitting locks   121
Cabinet bases   123

**4 DRAWERS, HANDLES AND
BOXES   126**
Drawer making   126
Drawer framing   134
Handles   135
Box constructions   138
Box hingeing   143
Glass and mirrors   145

APPENDICES   147
A   Sawing boards   147
B   The rip tenon saw   148
C   An aid to groove mitre joints by
    router   150
D   An aid to groove mitre joints on the
    circular saw   151
E   Glueing up mitred boxes   152
F   An aid to make keyed mitre joints for
    boxes   153
G   A device to construct comb (or finger)
    joints on the sawbench   154
H   Drawer slip cramps   155
I   Diminishing dovetails   156

BIBLIOGRAPHY   157

INDEX   158

INTRODUCTION

I cannot remember not having some of the basic woodworking skills. However, many men, women, boys and girls, of all ages, who are keen to make a start at woodworking, find that a multitude of excellent books on the craft assume very basic knowledge which they do not have.

This is really a pre-textbook. It is aimed mainly at those working alone. The apprentice has the guidance of a master craftsman, while the college student has tutors. Keen amateurs, often working in total isolation, lack this advantage. It is hoped that this book will start them off soundly, so that they will soon be able to take full advantage of good technical books, some of which are listed in the bibliography; and if not designing original work, beginners will be competent to work from books of designs, drawings and magazine articles.

Unfortunately, as is the case with other crafts, the initial skills needed are the most difficult to acquire. Planing a flat surface, for a beginner, is much more difficult than cutting a secret mitre dovetail for a more experienced worker.

Accurate joints cannot be marked out and later cut using components which are in twist, unsquare and of uneven thickness. Accurate planing is the foundation upon which successful constructions are built. It is not sufficient to watch a craftsman planing and then to attempt to copy him. He is not just standing beside a plane and moving it back and forth. It is necessary to realize that he is doing much more than that. If the craftsman is not there to ask, the beginner needs to be given a description of what he is doing and what it feels like. Unlike metal, wood is not uniform. Every piece is different, and herein lies much of the attraction and the charm of working with wood. Each piece requires individual attention and the worker is rewarded by the endless variation of grain pattern and ultimate finish.

Observing many student disasters over the years I have come to realize that lack of skill is the cause of remarkably few of them. This is because, time not being money, amateurs can proceed so slowly and by such small steps that success is almost guaranteed. They can, for instance, examine the wood after almost every shaving. In this way it is virtually impossible to plane undersize. The main causes of failure seem to be careless and faulty marking out (often even just not bothering to shade in or indicate the waste), or else blunt tools: that extra turn of the plane's adjusting screw, that results in tearing by the blunt cutter; the extra force needed for a blunt chisel with the resulting reduction of control, or the slow wandering progress of a blunt saw. Hence before any activity can begin the tools must be properly prepared and sharpened.

It was difficult to decide which constructions to include as 'basic'. Finally, I selected those traditional and proven joints and constructions for the four basic cabinet-making forms. These are the stool or table construction, the carcase or box construction, the door and the drawer. Almost all furniture is made up from these units in varying combinations.

A number of small power tools is now available to the amateur. These have made possible several quite acceptable alternatives to traditional jointing, and this book takes account of them.

During the last few years in British schools we have seen the abandonment of the 'O' and 'A' level examinations in Woodwork and their replacement by the 'progressive' Craft, Design and Technology. In the post-war years fine cabinet making was produced in many schools by well-trained and gifted teachers, particularly so in the grammar schools which produced future teachers. Alas, pupils now emerging from the schools who opt for further education in woodworking crafts are sadly deficient in basic skills. It is hoped that this book satisfies the real needs of such people.

In spite of the non-sexist trends in the schools it is a fact that girls emerge even more deficient in woodworking skills than boys. Several outstanding women cabinet makers have shown that they can more than hold their own with men. I hope this book will fill that gap and increase the confidence of girls and women.

Chapter 4 on drawer construction was written many years ago by my former tutor Cecil Gough who has generously permitted me to use it. Over the years I have found that it cannot be improved on. Some of the material has previously appeared in abridged form in *Woodworker* magazine. The Editor has kindly agreed to its inclusion.

I am much indebted to the hundreds of pupils and students with whom I have worked over many years, who have brought to my attention, often unwittingly, the problems of the beginner. I hope I have solved a good proportion of them. While I am sure that many readers will enjoy the book in an armchair by the fire, its real place is propped up on the bench like a music score, and if it eventually falls to pieces there it will have achieved its purpose.

Metric conversions are approximate, in round numbers, although where it is vital the conversions are accurate.

1 BASIC WOODWORKING SKILLS

Planing

One cannot overemphasize the importance of good plane management. It was the plane which made possible the development from the carpenter—whose main tools were the axe, the adze and the saw—to the joiner, cabinet maker, chair maker, musical instrument maker and all those other craftsmen in wood who require components produced to precise limits and with a fine finish.

The best machine planing still needs hand finishing to remove the ripples. In spite of machine makers' claims, sanding will never produce components accurately to size, nor will it remove tears put in by poor planing. It is equally unsound to think that poor planing can be rectified by scraping. Not only is the latter laborious in both working and sharpening, but truly flat surfaces can never be produced in this way. In short, there is no substitute for a well-sharpened and finely adjusted hand plane.

Stripping the plane

In order fully to understand the working of the metal plane it is a good idea, particularly for the beginner, to strip down the plane to its smallest component. If you have an old or secondhand plane this is a good opportunity to renovate it. Even if the plane is misassembled and maladjusted, no damage can be done to it. Figure 1 shows the structure quite clearly and gives the correct names to all the components. It will be seen that there are three distinct adjustments.

The depth of cut, that is the thickness of shaving removed, is controlled by the cutter adjusting wheel. The wheel running up and down a left-hand thread operates the Y lever. This in turn engages in the Y lever socket of the cap iron (or breaker), which it moves up or down. The blade is secured to the cap iron and is moved by it.

The second adjustment is lateral. The lateral lever has a circular stud at its end. When the plane is assembled it must be made certain that this stud fits into the slot in the blade. Movement of the lever thus moves the cutting edge sideways, preventing one corner from digging in.

The third adjustment is commonly called closing or opening the mouth. The whole frog is moved forward with the blade and the effect is to alter the size of the gap in front of the blade. The lever cap screw should be just sufficiently tight to make sideways movement of the blade with the fingers difficult but not impossible.

Sharpening

All the edge tools are unfit for use when new. They have been ground by the makers on a coarse grindstone and require a better edge for use on wood. This is obtained by sharpening (or honing) the tool on an oilstone which gives it a much finer and keener edge. For

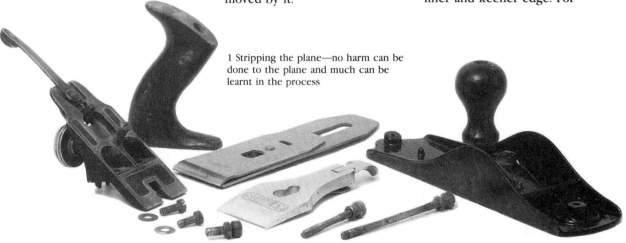

1 Stripping the plane—no harm can be done to the plane and much can be learnt in the process

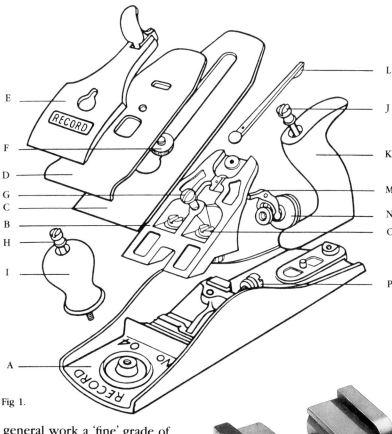

Fig 1.

Fig 1. Adjustable iron plane. **A**—Body, **B**—Frog, **C**—Cutting iron, **D**—Cap iron, **E**—Lever cap, **F**—Cap iron screw, **G**—Lever cap screw, **H**—Knob nut and screw, **I**—Knob, **J**—Handle nut and screw, **K**—Handle, **L**—Lateral adjusting lever, **M**—Y adjusting lever, **N**—Cutter adjusting wheel, **O**—Frog screws, **P**—Frog adjusting screws.

a small wooden gauge is helpful for this (Fig 4). Slightly oil the stone with a thin machine oil. Commence sharpening by using the full length of the stone and rubbing until the smallest burr or wire edge is formed along the entire width of the tool (Fig 5). The wear to the stone can be more evenly spread if the stone is housed in an unorthodox case (Fig 6). Remove from the guide and place flat on the stone by stages (Fig 7). Keeping the tool dead flat, rub off the burr, some of which will remain. A few light strokes alternately with the bevel up and down will remove most of the burr. For a really keen edge the process can be briefly repeated on a fine natural stone. Finish off by stropping on a piece of thick

general work a 'fine' grade of artificial stone is suitable. If a very keen edge is needed, a much more expensive natural stone can be used for finishing off.

The common grinding angle is 25° (Fig 2). Generally this angle is increased to 30° on the oilstone. Fig 3 shows this on a wide chisel. For the beginner there is no better way of working than with a sharpening guide such as the Eclipse model (see photographs 2 and 3). After considerable practice some workers will dispense with this tool, but even for the most skilled it remains valuable for narrow chisels and blades, and when a straight and square plane cutter is required.

Clamp in the tool, projecting the recommended distance × –

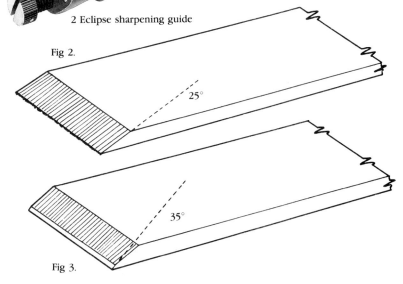

2 Eclipse sharpening guide

Fig 2.

25°

Fig 3.

35°

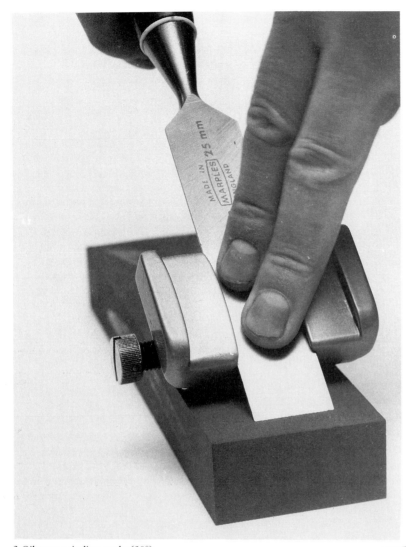

plane requires virtually no curvature, but the corners should be slightly rounded (Fig 9) to prevent them 'digging in'. This is achieved during the sharpening by giving a little extra finger pressure at each corner.

There is a life-cycle to the cutting edge of a tool (Fig 10). Each time it is sharpened the oilstone bevel becomes larger and the angle less acute. After a while there is so much metal to remove that the sharpening process becomes inconveniently long and the angle is considerably more than 30°. It is now time to regrind the tool and start again. Regrinding back to 25° can be carried out on a vertically running natural stone cooled with water, an oil-cooled, horizontally running stone, or a high-speed carborundum-type wheel. In the case of the latter great care must be taken, by frequent dipping out in water, not to overheat the cutting edge and so destroy its hardness.

After re-grinding, the size of the oilstone bevel must be kept to the minimum to save both sharpening time and metal.

3 Oilstone grinding angle (30°)

Fig. 4. Gauge used with sharpening guide.

leather glued to a wood strip (Fig 8) and dressed with finest automobile valve grinding paste. It cannot be emphasized too strongly that the flat side of the tool must remain absolutely flat, with no trace of a bevel on this flat side.

Plane cutters require a slight modification. The cutter of the jack plane requires a slight curvature across the entire width (1–1.5mm (1/16in.) is about right). The smoothing

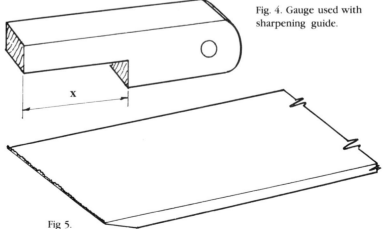

x

Fig 5.

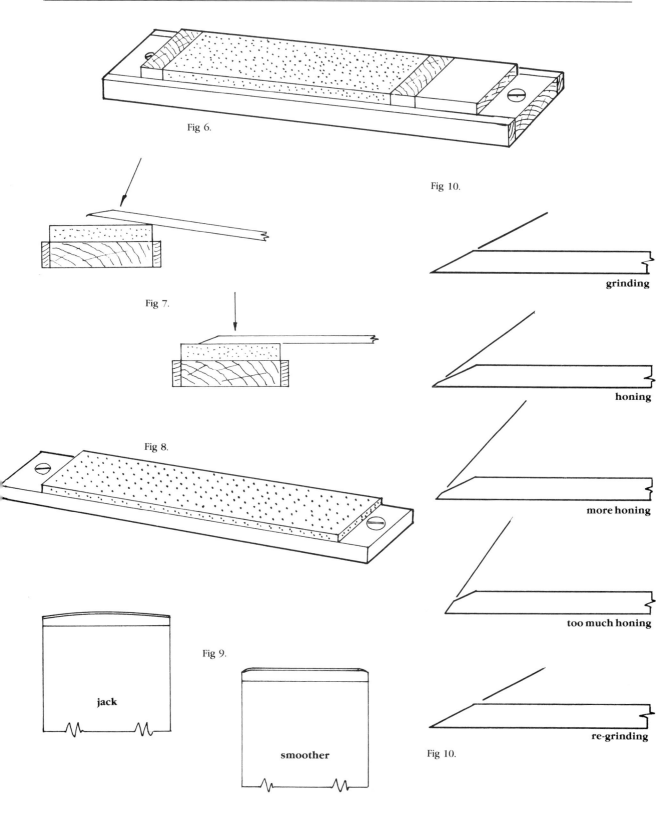

Fig 6.

Fig 7.

Fig 8.

Fig 9.

jack

smoother

Fig 10.

grinding

honing

more honing

too much honing

re-grinding

Fig 10.

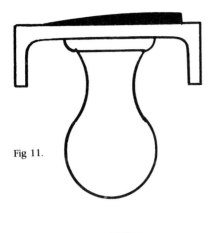

Fig 11.

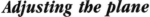

Fig 12.

Adjusting the plane

A metal plane will need to be carefully adjusted at the start of each session of work, and each time the blade has been sharpened. Before adjusting the plane itself, the cap iron or breaker must be adjusted. This will be dealt with in more detail later, but for general work the cap iron should be set at about 1mm (1/16 in.) from the cutting edge. With the cap iron properly fixed the main adjustment can take place. For this a piece of mild, clear softwood is needed of about 13mm ($\frac{1}{2}$ in.) thickness. This is held edge upwards in the vice.

Look down the sole of the plane (see photograph 4). It helps to have a piece of white paper on the bench to sight onto. Observe the cutting edge (Fig 11), and by means of the lateral lever adjust the blade until it appears symmetrical (Fig 12). This is a provisional adjustment only. Next, with the cutter adjusting wheel, fully withdraw the blade. Now start to plane on the softwood strip. Nothing will happen. Take up the slack and slowly increase the cut, still planing. When the first very fine shaving appears, stop. Observe this shaving very carefully; it should come from the centre of the blade, the two corners of the blade should not cut. If one corner does cut, move the lateral lever slightly in the direction of the cutting corner, having first taken up the

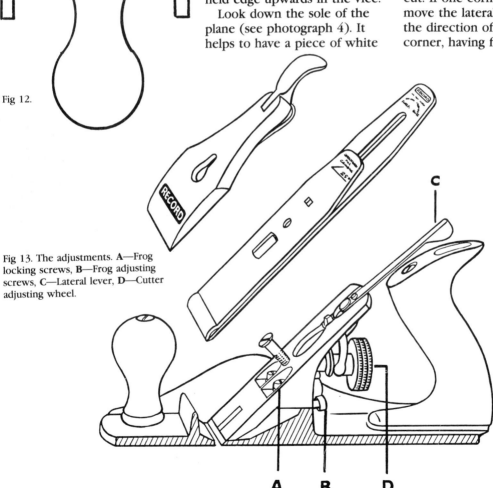

Fig 13. The adjustments. A—Frog locking screws, B—Frog adjusting screws, C—Lateral lever, D—Cutter adjusting wheel.

A   B   D

slack. Continue in this way until only the centre cuts. This lateral adjustment is the one which beginners usually find the most difficult.

The adjustment of cut is quite straightforward. To increase the cut, turn clockwise. To decrease the cut, turn anticlockwise, then clockwise, sufficiently to take up the slack in the mechanism. Failure to take up the slack will result in the blade slowly creeping back during planing. Do not take too heavy a cut; two light cuts are always easier than one heavy one, and when extra strength is used accuracy is sacrificed.

The final adjustment is the size of the mouth (Fig 13). Two frog locking screws (A) are slackened and the frog is moved back or forward by the frog adjusting screw (B). Unfortunately this will upset the lateral adjustment which must be done again. The purpose of this adjustment is to avoid 'tearing'.

There are five cures for tearing:
1. Reverse the direction of planing.
2. Sharpen the blade.
3. Take a very fine cut.
4. Set the cap iron very close.
5. Close up the mouth.

Any one of these or a combination of any number of them will prevent tearing. On the other hand too close a cap iron and too fine a mouth will cause 'clogging'. It is always worth examining the mouth as this may be poorly formed or obstructed by a blob of paint, which can be removed by gentle filing.

4 The adjustment is made easier by sighting down onto a piece of white paper

How to plane

Planing is not a difficult technique and, like swimming, once learnt is never forgotten. However it is not enough merely to watch someone planing and to try to copy what they do. The beginner needs to know what is being attempted and how this is being achieved.

Make a start by using a really sharp cutter, carefully adjusted as just described. To start, take a piece of clear, knot-free softwood about 25mm (1in.) thick and about 300mm (12in.) long and grip it edge up in the vice.

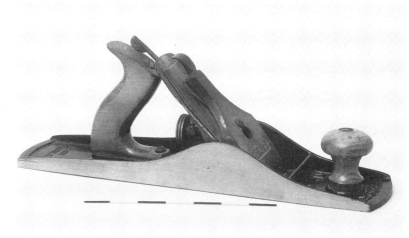

6 The 2 3/8 in. jack plane. A general purpose bench plane

Now stand correctly (see photograph 5). The left foot should be perpendicularly below the near edge of the vice. It should be at an angle of approximately 45° to the front of the bench. The right foot will position itself at a convenient distance away, more or less at right angles to the bench (Fig 14).

Before trying to plane, settle the front of the plane on the job. This is vital. The jack plane (see photograph 6) has quite a sizeable piece of sole in front of the mouth. This must be felt to be well settled in firm contact with the work. Next feel for the catch of the blade; to do this, gently move the plane forward

7 Planing—help can be given to a beginner to keep the plane settled on the wood

Fig 14.

until you can feel the blade touching the wood.

Now push forward steadily. Do not draw back the plane to take a swing at it. Do not disturb the 'settled' front. A beginner or a child will find it helpful to keep the right elbow well tucked in and to push using a body motion, as one would if trying to push the bench. When more skill has been developed, more of an arm movement may be employed. This method of planing with the arm tucked in will continue to

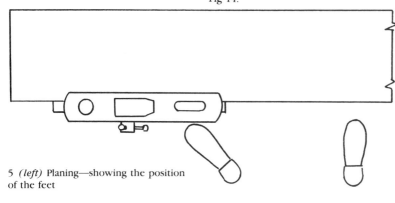

5 (left) Planing—showing the position of the feet

8 Planing—the start of the stroke. Strong downward pressure is put on the front of the knob

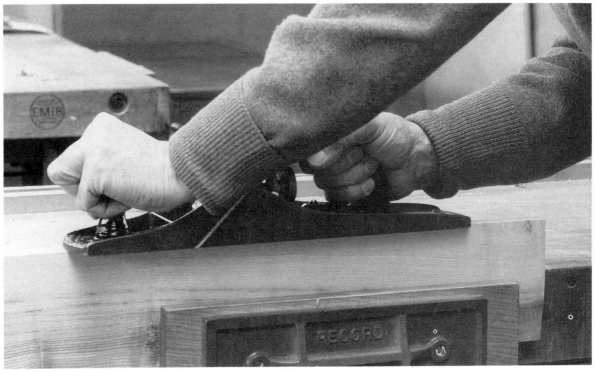
9 Planing—mid-stroke. Equal downward pressure on both handles

be useful for great accuracy and when the wood is unusually hard. It is particularly difficult to maintain the necessary downward pressure when the plane is at arm's length.

The correct downward pressure is of great importance for successful planing. At the start of the stroke there is strong pressure by the left hand, on the knob (Fig 15), while the right hand on the handle pushes straight forward. In the middle of the stroke the down pressure is equal by both hands. At the end of the stroke the positions are reversed, in order to stop the plane from tipping off the end. Now the front knob provides the forward motion while the handle gives the downward pressure. Practise this, aiming to produce full-

Fig 15.

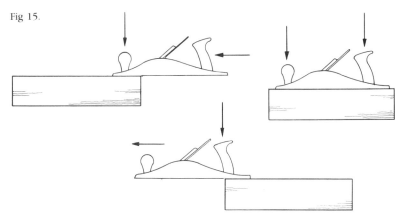

length, full-width shavings. Remember that two thin shavings are easier to push than one thick one. Keep to a thin shaving for all early practising.

These instructions will naturally be reversed for left-handed readers, who should fit the vice at the opposite end of the bench. Any reader

undecided whether to work left- or right-handed is advised to settle for right-handed working, as specialist planes will be encountered at a later stage which cannot conveniently be worked left-handed.

The friction of a steel plane is considerably greater than that of a wooden one. Consequently

10 Planing—completing the stroke by strong downward pressure on the rear handle

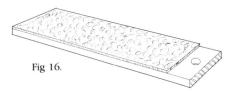

Fig 16.

some form of lubrication is needed to reduce the effort required. This commonly takes the form of a candle stump, although a better method is to use an oilpad (Fig 16). This not only does not get lost or trodden on, but also serves as a safe parking place when the plane is not in use, both lubricating the sole and protecting the cutting edge from damage. The old folk custom of laying the plane on its side dates back to the days of all-wooden planes with hammer-driven wedges. To do this with modern metal planes tends to upset the carefully adjusted lateral setting.

Make the oilpad by glueing a strip of carpet to a wooden base. Do not use rubber-backed carpet. Dress with a thin machine oil. Once the pad is in condition, a piece of paper wiped across it should be only slightly soiled. Too much oil will mark the wood and also pick up a lot of workshop dirt and dust. A hanging hole completes the job.

Direction and length of plane

'Against the grain' is an expression commonly used but understood by few but woodworkers, all of whom have experienced wood tearing to produce a poor finish instead of cutting sweetly. If the construction of the timber is imagined as being like a bundle of drinking straws lying generally at a slight angle (Fig 17), it will be clear that a stroke made in the direction of B will cut cleanly as in sharpening a pencil, while one cut in the direction of A will cause the straws to crumble in advance of the cut. Try sharpening a pencil this way with the pencil held in the vice.

An indication of the way the fibres lie is given by the grain pattern on the sides (Fig 18). Observe this pattern and plane 'uphill'. Often the grain pattern is horizontal (Fig 19) and in this case planing can be either way. The steeper the angle, the more necessary it is to plane uphill. Sometimes the pattern reverses (Fig 20). This is termed 'cross grained' and extra steps have to

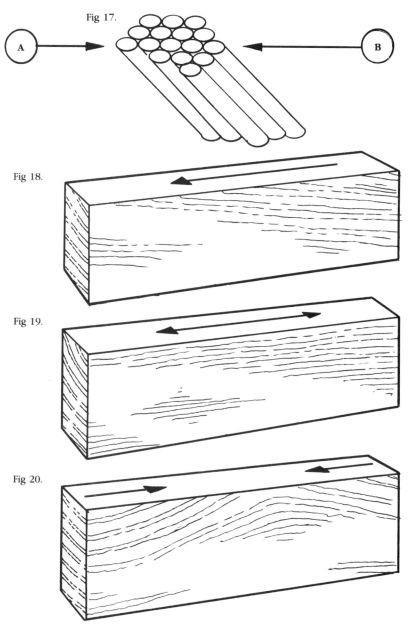

Fig 17.

Fig 18.

Fig 19.

Fig 20.

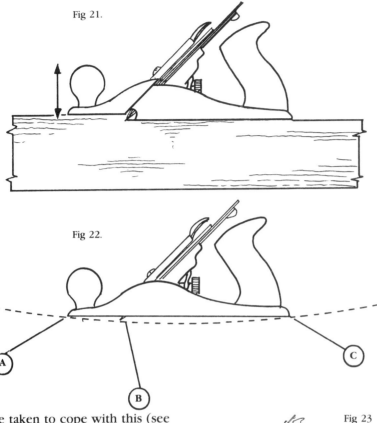

Fig 21.

Fig 22.

A

B

C

work on a small area without having to plane down a much larger area to get rid of a blemish.

This apparent disadvantage is made use of in preparing the true face. Particularly when a beginner attempts to do straightforward planing, there is a good chance of the work becoming rounded, that is high in the middle. By deliberately planing hollow (as described in Chapter 6) then planing through to get a full-length shaving, very great accuracy can be achieved.

End grain

Planing end grain presents problems to the unwary. If the end of a board on which it is wide enough to settle a plane is planed right through, the end fibres will inevitably split off, and more will split off with each stroke. This is called 'spelching' (Fig 24). Fortunately there are three possible remedies for this, with the most convenient being chosen for the particular circumstances.

The board can be planed towards the centre in both directions (Fig 25). If the end grain is to be polished and seen, planing both ways can sometimes produce two different shades or textures with a clear join between them. This is avoided (Fig 26) by chiselling off the far corner so a minimum amount of waste is required for this (Fig 27a or b). In order to secure an adequate amount of waste, it is sometimes desirable to plane both ends to length before finally planing to width.

If this is not feasible a block can be glued to the end, sometimes with a paper joint, and the angle cut off this in the same manner (Fig 28). With

be taken to cope with this (see 'Cures for tearing' p.13). Though the grain pattern on the side is not an infallible guide, it is generally correct.

To plane a flat surface with a woodworker's plane is theoretically impossible. It could only be done if the plane had a movable sole in front of the mouth (Fig 21) in the manner of a planing machine. The cutter would line up exactly with the main rear sole. The front sole would then be raised by the thickness of the cut. Such a plane would be enormously expensive to produce. As it is we have a plane as in Fig. 22. The front end, the blade and the rear end are respectively marked A, B and C. It is a fact of geometry that only one circle will pass through points A, B and C so, again in theory, the

Fig 23

plane is designed to plane a shallow curve. It follows then that the longer the plane the closer that curve is to a straight line (Fig 23).

When producing components to size, the jack plane is used. For great accuracy, when planing edge joints on boards, the much longer trying plane is used (see photograph 27 p.59). When we are only cleaning up prior to polishing, and great accuracy is not required, the shorter smoothing plane (see photograph 25 p.54) allows

19

forethought this can be done last thing at night to avoid a long wait. Alternatively the block can be held temporarily in place with a sash cramp.

All end grain planing needs a particularly sharp and finely set blade, a well-lubricated sole and plenty of downward pressure.

Two planing exercises

The aim of the following exercises is to produce full-length, full-width shavings. The first exercise will show whether the reader is achieving this aim.

Grip in the vice, edge upwards, a piece of clear softwood about 300 × 75 × 25mm (12 × 3 × 1in.). With a soft woodworker's pencil draw a line down the middle (Fig 29). Using a sharp, well-adjusted plane, plane a full-length, full-width shaving. The pencil mark should be completely removed. Mark the wood with the pencil and plane again, repeat this for ten shavings. If a trace of the pencil mark remains, begin the count again. After ten successful attempts have a brief rest then cut a further ten. This is the technique of planing when the wood is narrower than the plane.

When the wood is wider than the plane, the technique is modified as follows. Grip in the vice a similar piece of wood about 75mm (3in.) wide. Clean the dirt and roughness from one of the wide surfaces and draw on it three pencil lines (Fig 30). Proceed to plane as before, in groups of three shavings, either left side, right side and centre or left, centre, right. After three cuts, if all trace of the pencil mark is gone, the score is one. Continue in groups of three as before up to ten. Start again if a trace of pencil remains. It is not necessary to take off a line with each cut, but after three cuts all the lines must be gone. Repeat as before for a second group of ten.

If the wood is wider still a group of four, five or more cuts will be necessary. The important thing is that the planing must be regular and consistent.

Fig 24.

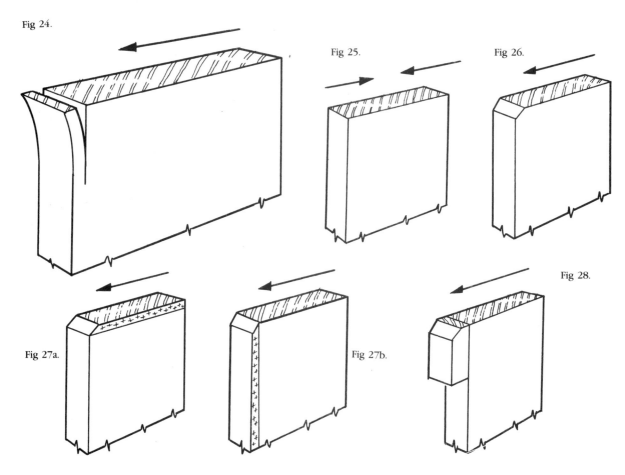

Fig 25.

Fig 26.

Fig 27a.

Fig 27b.

Fig 28.

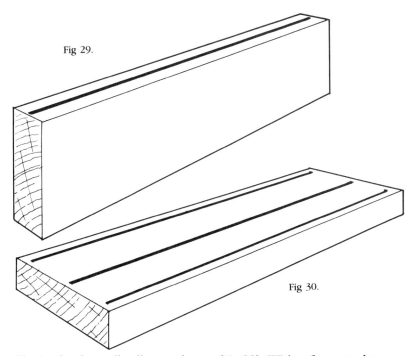

Fig 29.

Fig 30.

Planing haphazardly all over the board will never produce a flat surface.

Facing

Just as a building requires a true and accurate foundation from which all the subsequent measurements can be taken, so every piece of wood requires one accurate surface from which sizes and angles can be taken later on. This is known as the *true face* (often confusingly called the 'face side'). There is a straightforward method of obtaining the true face, which can be tried out on a softwood piece of about 300 × 75 × 25mm (12 × 3 × 1in.).

Grip the wood in the vice and plane off the dirt and roughness from one large side (Fig 31). Resist the temptation to clean up all sides—it may look nice but there is a good chance of ending up under the required size. Now make a thick, soft pencil mark at each end

(Fig 32). With a fine set plane try to plane the piece hollow. That is, start the cut just inside the first pencil mark and lift off just before the second.

Continue this process with a fine set until the plane no longer cuts. Failure will be shown by the removal of a pencil mark. If this happens replace the mark again and continue.

When the plane will cut no more, plane the wood from end to end. The first cut will remove a small shaving from each end, and subsequent shavings will get bigger. When a full-length shaving has been produced, *stop*, and test for accuracy (Fig 33). Naturally, if the workpiece is wider than the plane, groups of cuts will be taken in this way.

Tests for a true face

There are three tests for a true face:
1. Is the work flat in length? Test with a steel or wooden straightedge which must be longer than the work (Fig 34).
2. Is the work flat in width? Test

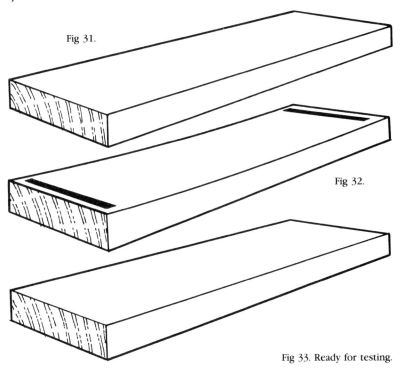

Fig 31.

Fig 32.

Fig 33. Ready for testing.

21

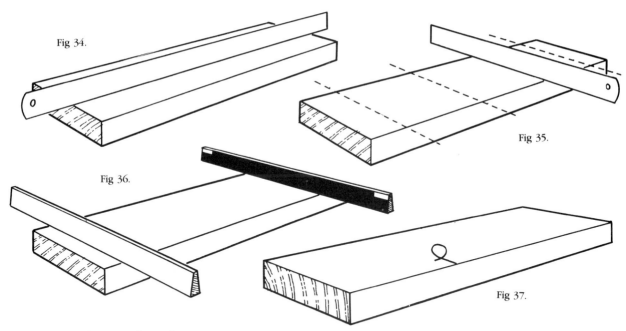

Fig 34.

Fig 35.

Fig 36.

Fig 37.

in several places with a rule (Fig 35).

3. Is the work 'in wind' (i.e. twisted)? Test with a pair of winding strips. Place a winding strip on at each end, step back a couple of paces then sight across the top of the winding strips. These magnify twist and quite a small error will be revealed (Fig 36).

Correct where necessary, then test again. Take care that in correcting for one of these tests, one or both of the others is not disturbed. When all the tests have been satisfactorily passed, put on a pencil face mark (Fig 37).

For some constructions the true face is inwards, others require it on the outside. It is important to bear this in mind when examining the timber before facing. In other words, does the best-looking surface have the true face or not?

Edging

The *true edge* (sometimes called the 'face edge') is the next

important stage in producing material to size. The work already faced is held in the vice edge upwards and preferably with the true face outwards

(Fig 38). This latter will of course depend on how the grain runs. The process is similar to that of facing. Clean the dirt and roughness from the

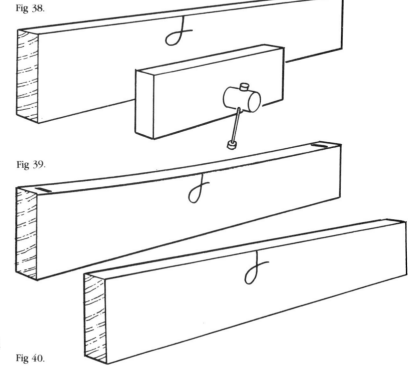

Fig 38.

Fig 39.

Fig 40.

edge on which the face mark stands. Make a strong pencil mark at each end (Fig 39). Plane as previously to hollow the workpiece between the marks, continuing until the plane no longer cuts. Now plane right through, stopping when the first full-length, full-width shaving results (Fig 40).

Tests for a true edge

1. Is the work flat in length? Test with a straightedge longer than the work (Fig 41).
2. Is the work flat in width? Test with a rule; if the last shaving was full width the work will be flat in width automatically (Fig 42).
3. Is the edge square (i.e. at 90°) to the true face? Test with a try-square in several places (Fig 43).

Correct where necessary and mark with a 'vee' pointing to the true face (Fig 44). Often a cross is used which is not so useful. If the face mark is lost the 'vee' indicates which side it was. If the edge mark is lost the face mark does the same.

Edge planing

When the test for squareness has been made (Fig 45), it is more than likely that one side of the wood will be higher than the other. The obvious remedy appears to be to tilt the plane. However, this will merely produce a second surface (Fig 46), making it even more difficult to settle the plane. It was stated earlier that the jack plane blade is sharpened to a curve and advantage will now be taken of this. With the plane correctly adjusted (Fig 47), a shaving cut in the centre of the plane will be of an equal thickness across its width. A shaving cut near the edge of the

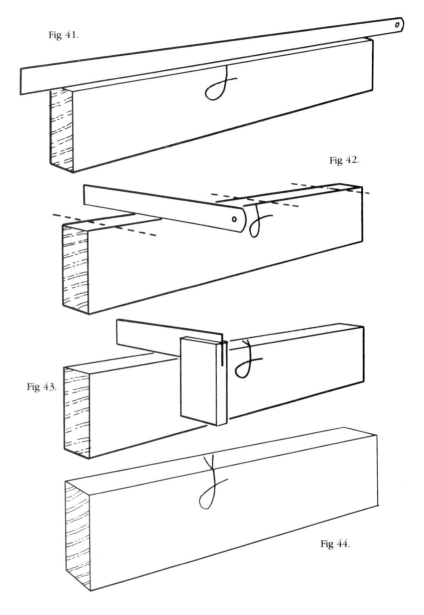

Fig 41.

Fig 42.

Fig 43.

Fig 44.

plane will have a thick side and a thin side, the latter thinning down to virtually nothing. Settle the plane on the workpiece (Fig 48). Successive shavings cut in this manner will gradually reduce the high side to squareness. The last shaving should be cut using the centre of the blade.

In order that the plane does not wander sideways during the

stroke the normal grip is replaced by the *edge grip*. The left hand no longer holds the front knob but instead grips the sole just behind it with thumb and first finger. The finger acts as a fence preventing sideways movement (see photographs 11 and 12). This is the standard method for planing all edges accurately.

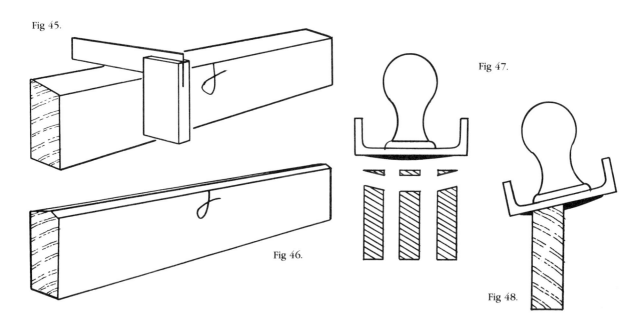

Fig 45.

Fig 46.

Fig 47.

Fig 48.

11 Planing—the edge grip. This is a way of avoiding the plane moving sideways

12 Planing—the edge grip. Here the fingers make a fence

Gauging

Gauging is the process of marking parallel lines which will later be sawn or planed. There is no substitute for the gauge when producing components accurately to size. There are two basic principles of gauging. One is that the pointer must 'trail'. The other is that almost all the pressure must be directed by the fence, onto the wood.

To learn to gauge, first put a length of wood in the vice, projecting about 50mm (2in.). Set the gauge to approximately the size required and tighten the screw finger-tight only, adjust to the correct size by tapping one or other end of the stem on the bench top then tighten the screw fully. The stock of the gauge is pushed by the thumb and further held with the index finger. The other fingers curl round the stem. The gauge is applied to the work on the flat side of the stem, the pointer well clear and the fence pushed against either the true face or the true edge. The gauge is slowly rotated (Fig 49) until the pointer just touches the wood and the pressure is taken on the corner of the stem. Maintain this angle and make a stroke, with the pointer trailing-fence firmly pressed into the work. Repeat on the end, the other long side and the other end. Always gauge from the true face or the true edge. If there is any doubt, shade the waste diagonally with a soft pencil.

Skilled workers will be seen holding the work by hand in a variety of peculiar ways. Beginners should use the vice wherever possible, learning first of all merely to gauge, then when proficient they can try out different methods of holding.

Narrow and thin pieces are best gauged in the vice as follows. Grip the wood by one end, with the true face (or true edge) outwards, and gauge until the gauge hits the vice (Fig 50). Slide through the vice to the position of Fig 51 and complete. Left-handers will find it convenient to reverse the stock and thus avoid having to push with the thumb against the screw.

When teaching children, a useful method is for the teacher to gauge one line then ask the pupils to do a further ten. Success is judged when the teacher's original line is indistinguishable from the rest. Many workers, particularly beginners, will find gauging easier if the hole for the gauge point is drilled at a slight angle to accentuate the 'trailing' effect described (Fig 52).

In order to end a gauge marking at a precise line and thus not show on the finished work, stab the point firmly into the finishing line (Fig 53). This small hole will clearly indicate the end of the gauging. Use the same method for the twin-point mortice gauge (considered later).

Fig 49.

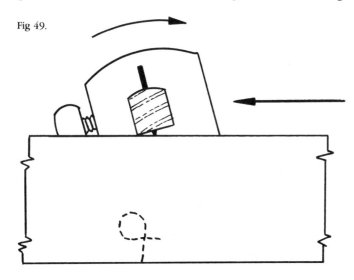

13 The current pattern marking gauge. A basic tool for which there is no substitute

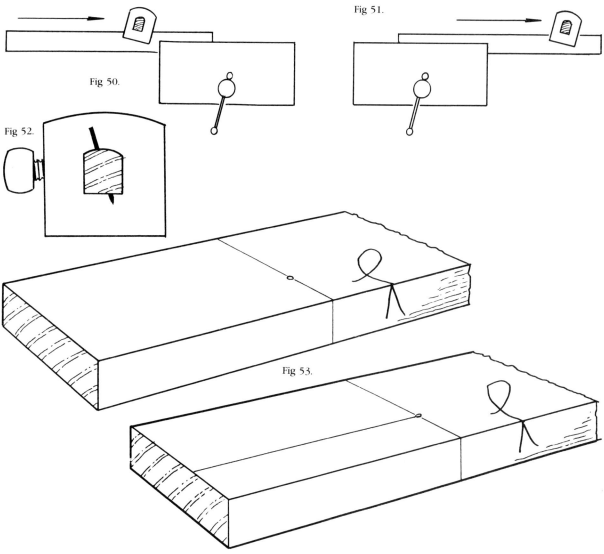

Fig 51.

Fig 50.

Fig 52.

Fig 53.

Producing to size

Before any marking out can be started the components must be brought accurately (and identically where necessary) to size.

Each component is first given a true face and a true edge, leaving two sides untouched (Fig 54).

Set the gauge to the required width and, working from the true edge, gauge the piece on four sides (Fig 55). If a soft, thick woodworker's pencil is run in the gauge line, two marks will be made (Fig 56). Plane down to the centre of the 'vee' groove made by the gauge, thus removing one of the two pencil marks. After some practice the pencil marking can be dispensed with. It is possible to plane down to the line all round the edges yet remain high in the centre; to check for this problem, apply a rule or straightedge (Fig 57). This process has produced three worked surfaces. The same process is repeated after gauging to thickness. It does not matter whether width or thickness is produced first. Often by planing to width first on a narrowish edge, a significantly wider surface is available for planing to thickness. When a large amount is to be removed saw off as much as possible first. Do not be disturbed by the somewhat untidy appearance of three of the corners (Fig 58).

While traces of the gauge mark remain, the component cannot possibly be undersize. In an actual job this would disappear in the final clean-up before polishing.

Beginners sometimes think that they will save time by

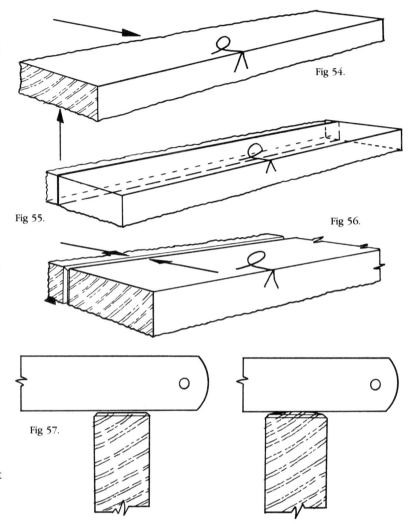

Fig 54.

Fig 55.

Fig 56.

Fig 57.

doing both gaugings first, followed by both planings, particularly when width and thickness are the same size. Reflection makes it obvious that planing to the mark A (Fig 59) will take off the gauge mark B. This will then have to be re-gauged, thus wasting more time than it was expected to save.

Summary

1. Make a true face.
2. Make a true edge.
3. Gauge to width.
4. Plane to width.
5. Gauge to thickness.
6. Plane to thickness.

It is equally suitable to do 5 & 6 before 3 & 4.

Squaring

Lines at right angles (across the grain) are marked with the try-square using a pencil, a ballpoint or a marking knife. No accurate marking can be done until a true face and a true edge have been produced and marked as such.

The cardinal rule is that the *stock* of the square should be

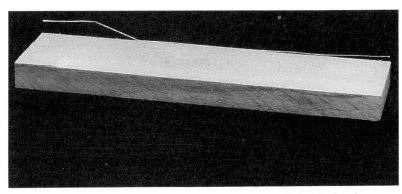

14 Producing to thickness. The gauge marking breaks away during the last fine shavings. Further planing will produce a piece undersize

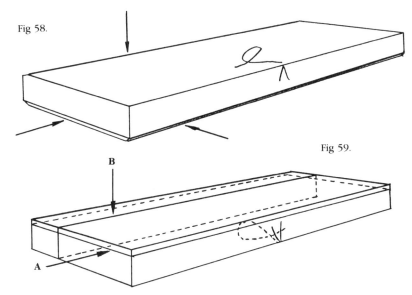

Fig 58.

Fig 59.

even if the sides are not parallel, and even if the square is slightly out of true.

When using a knife, time can be saved and accuracy improved by using the following simple technique. Mark the first line, turn the wood, put the knife edge in the knife cut (Fig 63) and slide the square up to it. The square can become out of true by wear from the knife (Fig 64), so check this periodically. The accuracy of the square needs occasional checking too. Plane a true edge on a wide board, preferably by machine, knife a line, reverse the square and repeat (Fig 65); any error will be evident.

Angles other than 90° can easily be marked and repeated as often as required by interposing a tapered block between the work and the square (Fig 66). This is much more reliable than the standard practice of using the sliding bevel which can so easily be knocked out of position. Shade the waste after squaring.

The marking knife is worth a moment's consideration. As sold, this often has a curved bevel on

against either the true face or the true edge (Fig 60). This gives eight possible positions. It does not matter whether or not the blade rests on a true surface. The full width of the stock should be used (Fig 60), not only part (Fig 61) since this can produce inaccuracies. If this rule is observed, the lines will finally meet (Fig 62A); if not a helix will result (Fig 62B) and the lines will never meet unless (and this cannot be assumed in hand work) opposite sides are perfectly parallel. Observing the rule, the lines will always meet,

Fig 60.

Fig 61.

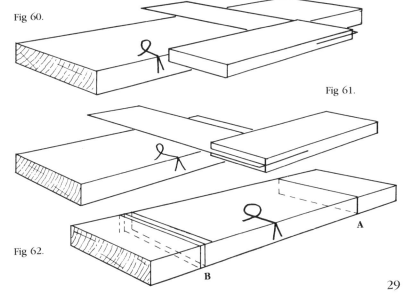

Fig 62.

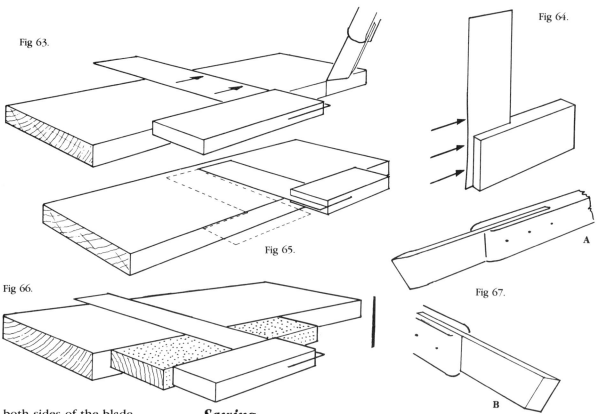

Fig 63.

Fig 64.

Fig 65.

Fig 66.

Fig 67.

A

B

both sides of the blade (Fig 67*A*). This should be re-ground with the bevel on one side only (Fig 67*B*). (Left-handers will, of course, grind the blade on the other side.) The knife is held like a pen, rather than like a dagger, and only the point is used; do not try to use the entire edge. The bevel should face away from the try-square, giving a vertical cut on the job side and a slope on the waste side. Of all the edge tools, this is the most neglected as far as sharpening is concerned. It is essential to keep it sharp.

The wood-handled knife is preferable to the combined knife and awl, especially for children. Facial injuries can result from the long, out-of-focus spike when the user is concentrating on the cut.

Sawing

This is the final skill the beginner needs to acquire in order to produce the component to the finished size required. It is also needed to cut the component to approximate size in the early stages.

The 250mm (10in) *tenon saw* is a convenient size. The work is held on a sawing board (see Appendix A). There are three ways of crosscut sawing

which for convenience may be called third-class, second-class and first-class sawing, according to the importance of the cut.

Third-class is for the early stages and for relatively unimportant work. Mark the cut line with pencil and shade the waste. Place the saw up to the line on the far corner but in the waste. Put the left-hand thumb against the saw and carefully draw back half a dozen times

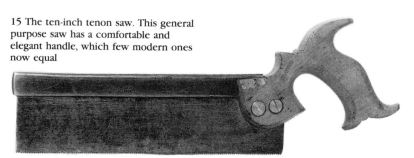

15 The ten-inch tenon saw. This general purpose saw has a comfortable and elegant handle, which few modern ones now equal

(Fig 68). Take the thumb away, stand well back from the work and hold the wood firm by leaning on it with the palm of the hand. This gives a much firmer hold than gripping between thumb and fingers. Now start to saw, gently lowering the handle to allow the sawcut to creep slowly across the face of the timber (Fig 69) until there is a sawcut 'kerf' the full width of the work. Then saw straight down and into the sawing board (which is expendable).

Second-class sawing is more precise. This time mark the cut line with the marking knife and try-square (Fig 70) and shade the waste. The knife severs the fibres and gives a better finish to the top edge of the cut. Hold the work in the vice and chisel

a small 'vee'-shaped nick on the further corner (Fig 71). The cut is vertical on the job side and sloping on the waste side.

Hold the piece firmly, or better still cramp it on a sawing board. Place the saw in the nick, draw back a few times then saw, again slowly lowering the handle (Fig 72), until the saw cuts the full width. Saw through to the sawing board.

First-class sawing is used for all really important work, particularly the shoulders of the mortice and tenon joint, and accurate work will already have been marked out with the knife. Deepen the knife cut right across the width of the piece. Holding it in the vice, chisel a shallow groove (Fig 73). This should be nibbled out with a wide chisel using tiny cuts for

which no appreciable strength is needed.

Cramp down firmly to prevent movement during sawing, preferably on a piece of waste wood or hardboard. Lay the saw in the groove, draw back a few times then saw through (Fig 74).

Bench sawing

Needless to say, the saw must be sharp and straight. A buckled saw will never cut a straight line, it will naturally want to produce its own curve. Your stance is also important. Hunching over the work is not conducive to good sawing. Stand well away, with the left arm straight, holding the work

Fig 71.

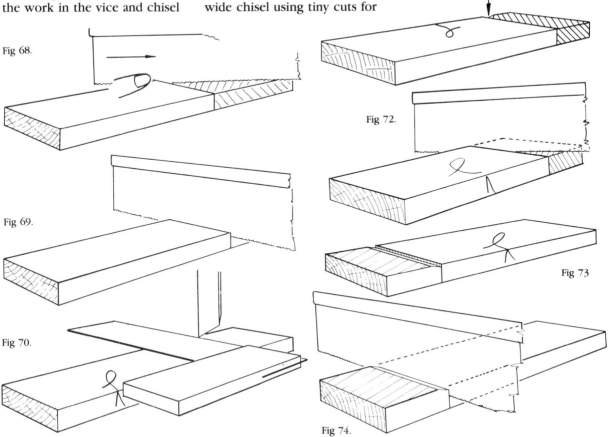

Fig 68.

Fig 69.

Fig 70.

Fig 72.

Fig 73

Fig 74.

by pushing with the palm rather than using a finger grip.

Some saw handles are not, as it may appear, designed for children. Only three fingers fit inside the handle the index finger should point along it, which helps to keep the saw on the right path. The wrist should remain rigid, preventing any movement of the saw out of the vertical. This is particularly important if the saw is large and wide. With a rigid wrist the pivots should be your elbow and shoulder. A sharp saw needs little downward pressure beyond its own weight, and only light pressure when sawing, producing a smooth and rhythmical stroke using the full length of the blade.

Two points are of importance when sawing. Lines across the grain which are cut to should be marked with the knife. Unlike the pencil, the knife line is of zero thickness. A chisel can be placed precisely in this mark if necessary, with no chance of error. Additionally the fibres are cleanly severed by the knife, giving a well-fitting appearance to a joint. The waste is shaded, not to prevent the job being thrown away and the waste kept, but to prevent work being cut undersize. Unlike the knife which cuts with no waste the saw removes sawdust. This dust must come from the waste not from the job, hence the slogan for sawing: 'up to the line, but in the waste'.

Screwing

This is one of the most common methods of jointing components. It is interesting that while the British use the name 'screwdriver', the American term is 'turnscrew'.

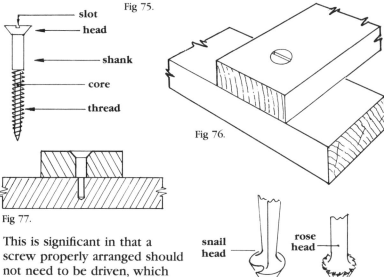

Fig 75.

Fig 76.

Fig 77.

Fig 78.

This is significant in that a screw properly arranged should not need to be driven, which implies hard work, but merely turned.

The screw has the following parts (Fig 75): head, shank, core and thread, and provision must be made for each of these in drilling the hole, since the screw, unlike the drill, cannot remove any wood. A standard screwed job (Fig 76) is one piece screwed directly to another and Fig 77 shows a section through the joint. The top piece needs a clearance hole made with a twist drill, in which the shank is free to turn. If this is too small much more effort will be required and the screw slot may be damaged, or the work may split if the hole is near the edge. The top piece may require countersinking. The correct tool for this is the snailhead countersink, but as an alternative the rosehead bit or

drill may be used (Fig 78); however this is inferior, being designed primarily for metal. A larger twist drill may be used, and this is most successful when used in a drilling machine with a depth stop.

The pieces can now be held in position with the screw dropped in place. A light tap on the screw will leave a dimple on the lower piece on which the next hole can be drilled. This is the pilot hole and its diameter is that of the screw *core*. The principle is that the drill makes room for the screw core and the thread bites into the sides of the hole, giving the greatest strength with the minimum effort.

The screwdriver end should be well maintained and the

Screw gauge		4	6	8	10	12
Clearance hole	in.	1/8	5/32	3/16	7/32	1/4
	mm	3	4	5	6	6.5
Pilot hole	in.	1/16	3/32	1/8	5/32	5/32
	mm	2	2	3	4	4

Fig 79.

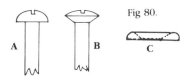

Fig 80.

A   B   C

blade must fit the slot. If allowed to become rounded it will slip out. Too large a blade will damage the wood, too small a blade will probably slip from the slot. Handles are made in proportion to blade size in order to exert the right pressure. Long, thin electrical screwdrivers should be used with particular care to avoid stripping the thread in the wood.

Fig 80 shows alternative screw heads. The round head is commonly used to secure fittings. If these are very thin a shallow clearance hole will be required for the shank before drilling the pilot hole. The raised head is sometimes used on metal fittings, and is most commonly used in industry. It can be conveniently used by the hand craftsman in conjunction with the screwcap washer when screwing plywood. The nature of plywood and sometimes its thinness makes it difficult to countersink neatly for a screw head.

For very small screws a four-sided awl is most convenient for the pilot hole. A touch of grease on a screw allows it to go in easier and by preventing rusting makes a later withdrawal easier too. Oak eventually has a corrosive effect on iron screws, so for good-quality work brass screws should always be used.

Boring

The making of holes with the brace and bit is still very common, in spite of the profusion of electric drills. The

drill is really a metal worker's tool and its cutting action is designed accordingly. It has a round shank which is held in the three-jaw chuck of the hand drill or electric drill (Fig 81). The main use of the *twist drill* is for making screw holes, having surplanted the collection of awls and gimlets which formerly did this job.

The woodworker's *brace* generally has only two jaws and the bit is provided with a square shank (Fig 82) to fit into a

square socket in the base of the chuck.

Although there is a great variety of *bits*, most of the commonly used ones conform to a pattern of which the centre bit (Fig 83) is the simplest. They all have a square shank to fit the brace, a sharp point to start precisely, a spur or nicker to sever the fibres and a router or cutter to remove the waste.

When boring shallow holes the best tool is the basic centre bit (see photograph 16). Grip

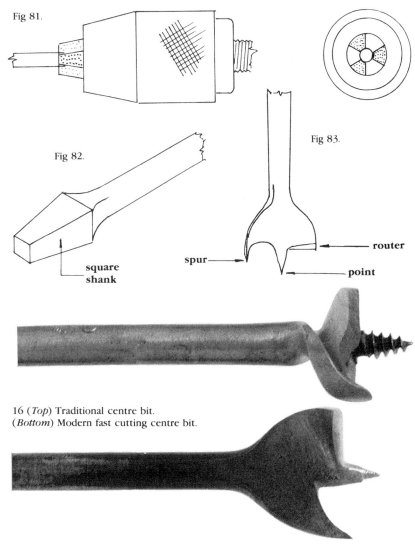

Fig 81.

Fig 82.

square shank

Fig 83.

spur

router

point

16 (*Top*) Traditional centre bit.
(*Bottom*) Modern fast cutting centre bit.

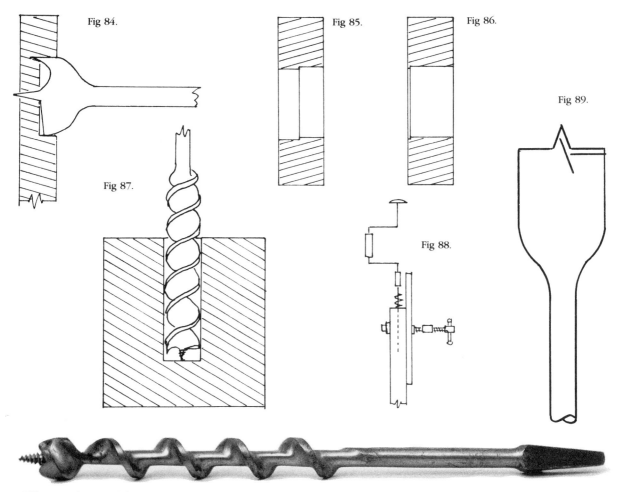

Fig 84.

Fig 85.

Fig 86.

Fig 89.

Fig 87.

Fig 88.

17 The twist bit—used for accurately guided deep holes

the work upright in the vice and bore with moderate pressure until the point comes through (Fig 84). Then, either reverse the work and bore from the other side, meeting somewhere in the middle (Fig 85) (the junction will always be slightly noticeable); or reverse the wood, score a circle with the spur and continue boring from the first side. This junction, being near the edge (Fig 86), is not so noticeable.

Deeper holes are bored with the twist bit (see photograph 17), or its shorter version, the dowel bit. This bit also has a needle point with a screw for applying the pressure, two spurs and two routers. In a deep hole (Fig 87), where the centre bit would wander sideways, the spiral of the twist bit, while preventing this tendency, also acts as an elevator to remove the shavings. Clockwise rotation brings up the shavings, anti-clockwise rotation sends them down the bit. When the required depth is reached (this can be marked by a piece of adhesive tape on the bit), turn the brace back and forth to break the thread in the wood. Then, turning clockwise, pull the bit out thus also bringing out all the waste and leaving a clear hole. To ensure correct alignment when boring deep holes, it is sometimes advisable to cramp a strip to the job (Fig 88) and sight against this.

The increasing popularity of the small hand-held electric drills has led in turn to the development of a special bit for use with them (Fig 89). This is the flat bit, which is used at high speed and has a scraping rather than a cutting action. Screw-nosed bits cannot be used in an electric drill because of its speed.

34

2 MAKING A TABLE OR STOOL

Construction and design

Design brief

Before commencing on any design other than a copy a *design brief* must be prepared. A design brief is a collection of all the data relevant to the construction and use of the article and the design is based on this information. The brief can best be produced by writing down as many questions as possible about the job, and then by experiment, research, measurement or judgement, find the answers to these questions. For example, questions about a coffee table might include the following:

Where will it be used?
Who will use it?
How many people will use it?
What will it carry?
How will people sit at it?
What will be its top shape?
How high will it be?
What will be its basic constructional form?
What will be the finish?
What wood is preferred or is available?
Will the top have any special finish?
Will a shelf or rack be required?

Design sketch

The answers to these practical questions will give the worker the length, the width and the height required. From these three figures a number of *design sketches* may be produced and the best one selected (Fig 90, for example).

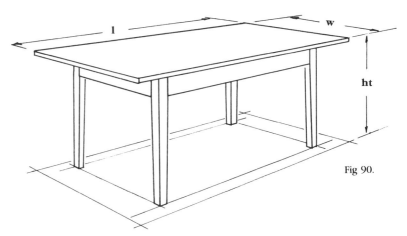

Fig 90.

Working drawing

From the design sketch it will now be possible to build up a *working drawing*. For items of coffee-table size a full-sized drawing is an advantage; larger items must of course be drawn to scale. These full-sized drawings can be drawn on decorator's 'lining' (ceiling) paper. Before making a start the following table of 'finished sizes' should be consulted (Fig 91).

sawn sizes		planed sizes	
mm	in.	mm	in.
100	4	96	3 7/8
75	3	71	2 7/8
63	2 1/2	59	2 3/8
50	2	46	1 7/8
38	1 1/2	34	1 3/8
32	1 1/4	28	1 1/8
25	1	21	7/8
19	3/4	15	5/8
15	5/8	11	1/2
12	1/2	8	3/8

Fig 91.

The sawn sizes are those used by the timber yards when sawing logs into boards. The finished sizes are those to which the sawn boards can be planed, either by hand or by machine. The first figure is both the maximum which can be obtained from the sawn board and also the size marketed as a planed board. In planning component sizes these sizes should be kept in mind in order to use wood with the greatest economy. A reduction of thickness of 1mm (1/16in.) may afford a considerable cost saving.

The working drawing (side view) (Fig 92) is built up as follows. Draw the ground line (*A*) then draw the top of the table (*B*). Consult the finished sizes and draw in the top thickness (*C*). Mark this off to length (*D*). Consider the overhang and draw in the outside edge of the legs (*E*). Consult the finished sizes again and draw in the leg thickness (*F*). The top rail (*G*) is drawn in next, wide enough to give a good joint but not wastefully wide. This can be made narrower if the extra support of a stretcher rail is given. The end (width) view can be similarly drawn. To save space this can be superimposed on the front view (shaded area).

When a proper mortice and tenon construction is to be used (as in this example) the length of the tenon must now be ascertained. This is easily done (Fig 93) by making a full-sized drawing on graph paper. Finally the inside edges of the legs can be tapered below the joint. This design retains the simplicity of an all-right-angle construction.

To obviate frequent reference to a drawing in the early stages it is convenient to produce a *cutting list* (Fig 94) and to work solely from this in the early stages.

Finished (i.e. final) sizes are used in the list, which avoids allowances being added at several stages in the work. Unfortunately, although there are only three dimensions there are many more names for them, e.g. length, height, width, depth, broad, thick, and so on. The three to be used are length (the distance along the grain), thickness (the smallest dimension) and width (the intermediate size). Width and thickness are often the same size.

To avoid confusion components are often lettered, as in the first column. The remaining columns are self-explanatory except for the blank one. A tick here signifies that the component has been sawn out. A cross tells that the piece has been produced to size ($\sqrt{}$) and is ready for marking out.

Marking out the joints

In a table or stool construction either the legs or the rails may be marked out first. This example starts with the rails. Cramp together the long and short pairs, with true faces out and true edges down. Mark each end with a knife and square (Fig 96). Then uncramp the pairs, square round the lines (Fig 97), and carefully saw off the waste. It is important to saw this cleanly in order to be able to gauge nicely on the end later. First gauge the set-in, at about 3mm (1/8in.), and then the haunch (Fig 98). The set-in is purely cosmetic, to conceal

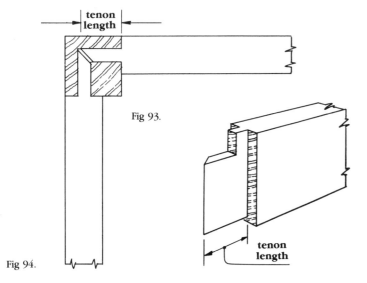

Fig 92.

Fig 93.

Fig 94.

tenon length

tenon length

CUTTING LIST			*All finished sizes in inches*				
NAME a. READER			JOB	COFFEE TABLE			
	PIECE	No.	L	W	Th.		REMARKS
A	Top	1	36	18	5/8	√	Oak/Jointed
B	Legs	4	18	1 3/8	1 3/8	√	Oak
C	Long rails	2	27 3/8	2 3/4	7/8	√	"
D	Short rails	2	13 3/8	2 3/4	7/8	√	"
E	Shrinkage buttons	16	EX	7/8	5/8		"

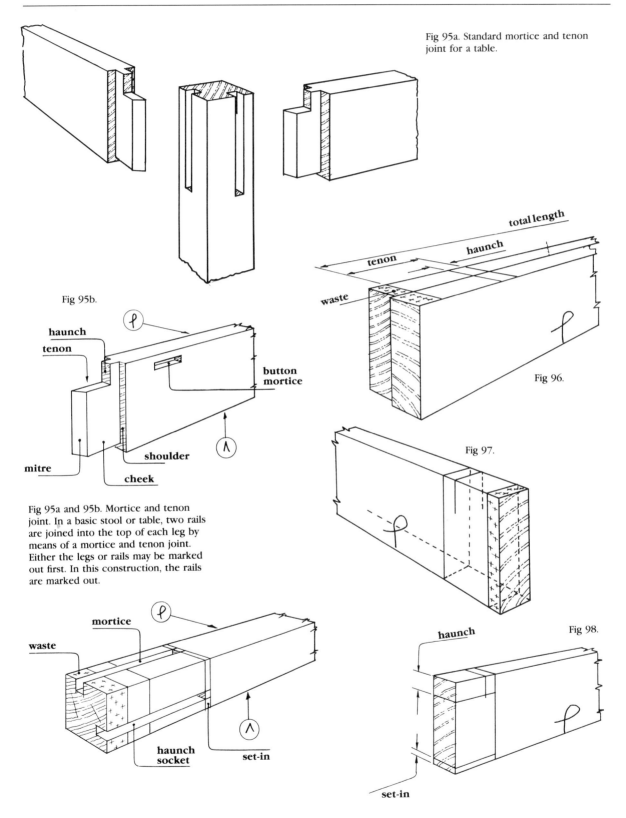

Fig 95a. Standard mortice and tenon joint for a table.

Fig 95b.

haunch
tenon

button
mortice

mitre

shoulder

cheek

Fig 95a and 95b. Mortice and tenon joint. In a basic stool or table, two rails are joined into the top of each leg by means of a mortice and tenon joint. Either the legs or rails may be marked out first. In this construction, the rails are marked out.

total length

tenon

haunch

waste

Fig 96.

Fig 97.

mortice

waste

haunch
socket

set-in

haunch

Fig 98.

set-in

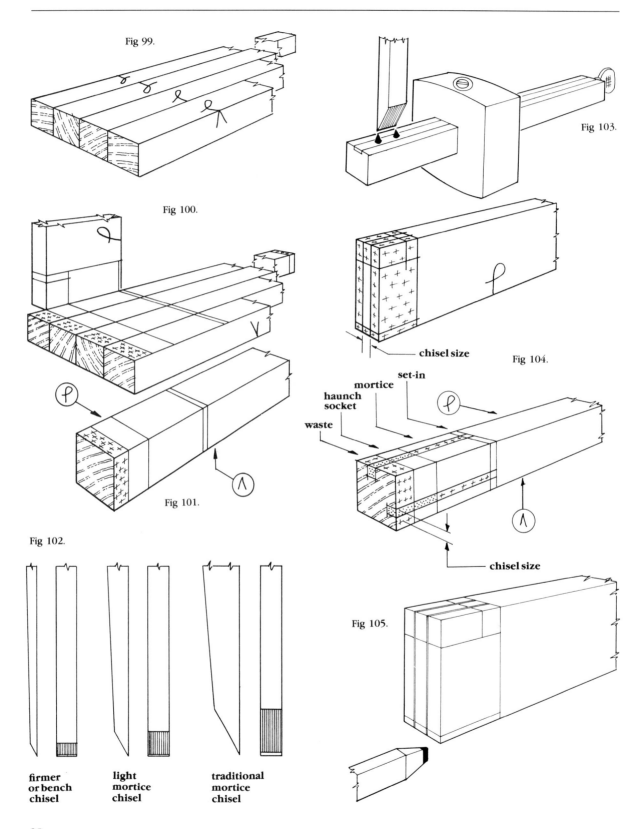

Fig 99.

Fig 100.

Fig 101.

Fig 102.

firmer
or bench
chisel

light
mortice
chisel

traditional
mortice
chisel

Fig 103.

chisel size

Fig 104.

waste

haunch
socket

mortice

set-in

chisel size

Fig 105.

18 Mortice gauge—essential for setting out mortice and tenon joints. This model is a combined mortice and marking gauge. The points must always be set to the chosen chisel and not to a rule

any irregularity in the joint. The haunch provides a bridge at the top of the leg, helping to prevent the mortice splitting and at the same time, by its added width to the tenon, reducing the possibility of the rail twisting in the leg. The haunch should be about a quarter of the tenon width. Some writers will say a third but this seems to reduce the tenon too much.

To mark out the legs, put them together with the faces and edges as shown (Fig 99) then turn them over and mark them on a blank face. Mark the total length, leaving some waste (which should be shaded) at each end. The waste must be

about 20mm ($\frac{3}{4}$in.) at the top or jointed end. Offer up the rail, and from it mark the haunch, set-in and rail width (Fig 100), square these across and uncramp. Square these lines onto the other blank face. The total length lines are squared right round (Fig 101).

The thickness of a tenon is normally about one third of the rail thickness. It is not taken from measurement but is the size of the nearest available chisel to this size. The traditional hand mortice chisels vary considerably from the nominal size. Machine chisels are quite accurate and are now becoming metric. Hand mortice chisels are much thicker than the common *firmer* or bench chisel (Fig 102), which is very liable to break when levering. The extra thickness of the mortice chisel is also a help in preventing it from twisting.

Set the mortice gauge carefully to the chisel (Fig 103) then set to its position on the rail, commonly central. Mark out the mortices on the legs (Fig 104), gauging from the true face and the true edge. Mark the tenons similarly, gauging from the true face.

Beginners will find it helpful later on, when sawing the tenons, if a thick, soft pencil is run in the gauge marks. This produces a double pencil mark (Fig 105). The waste should be very clearly marked with pencil, generally by diagonal shading. (The method adopted in the illustrations is to avoid confusion with the end grain, and is not typical.)

Note It is a good idea to number the joints to avoid confusion. This should be done on parts not involved in the cleaning-up process.

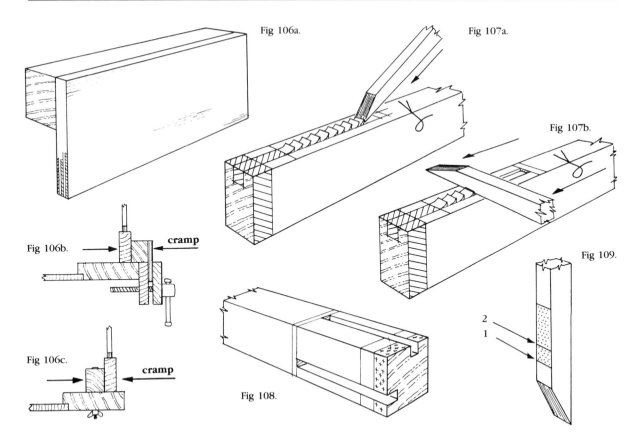

Fig 106a.

Fig 107a.

Fig 107b.

Fig 106b. ← cramp →

Fig 109.

Fig 106c. ← cramp →

Fig 108.

2
1

Chopping mortices

The mortices should be cut before sawing the tenons, as the latter are more liable to suffer accidental damage before assembly. It is not good practice to grip the work in the vice because then it cannot be tested for verticality, and if it is driven down in the vice during the process, it can become scored. Instead, cramp the work to a morticing block (Fig 106a) with G-cramps or handscrews. The block can be gripped in the vice (Fig 106b) or bolted to the bench (Fig 106c). This method is particularly useful when the bench has a front apron which

19 Chopping the mortice. The true mortice chisel is shown and the workpiece is cramped to a morticing block which is held in a bench vice

prevents cramping. The morticing block is useful when the workpiece is small and thin.

Fig 107a shows how a shallow trench can be cut before beginning the mortice proper. Simply lean on the chisel until there is a crunch, then wipe the chisel across (Fig 107b) removing the small chips. The chisel can now be positioned without effort. Before starting to chop, put a depth mark on the chisel (a piece of masking tape will do). If two mortices are to be cut (Fig 108), two depth marks are required (Fig 109). Do not cut the first mortice to full depth or the second will be chopped over a hole and the inside corner may break away (Fig 110). The first mortice should be chopped to a reduced

depth (Fig 111) then the second to full depth, thus avoiding this risk.

Having cramped the work securely to the block, drive in the chisel near one end of the mortice, bevel towards the centre (Fig 112). Check that it is vertical by placing a small straightedge against the true face (Fig 113); a longer rule will foul the handle. Withdraw the chisel, turn it round and drive in again with the bevel towards the hole. Push forward to break off the chip, then lever it out. Continue the sequence of *drive in* (Fig 114), *break off the chip* (Fig 115) then *lever out* (Fig 116). Continue almost to the end of the mortice, leaving a small piece of waste on which to lever. Frequently check that the chisel is vertical. Reverse

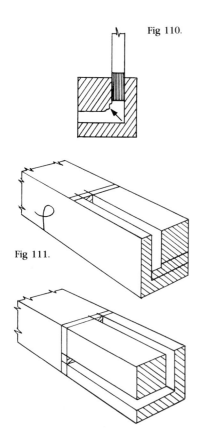

Fig 110.

Fig 111.

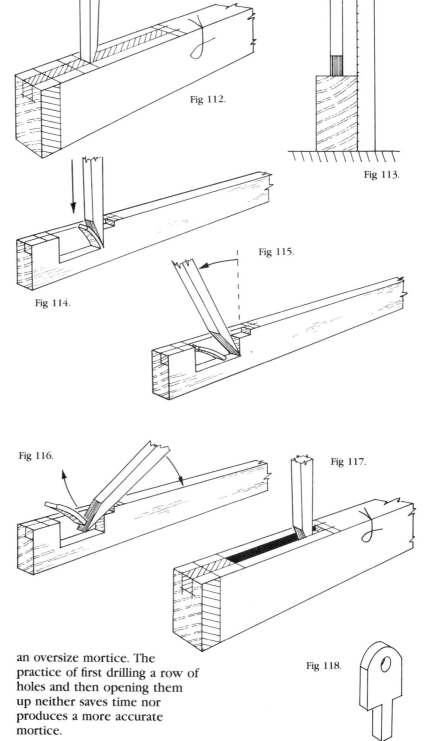

Fig 112.

Fig 113.

Fig 114.

Fig 115.

Fig 116.

Fig 117.

Fig 118.

the chisel and proceed to the other end. Continue the method, backwards and forwards until full depth has been reached (Fig 117). Finally chop down the ends at the knife marks, break off and remove the chip without bruising the ends.

Accuracy of depth can be tested by using an adjustable depth gauge or an improvized wooden one (Fig 118). If there is a haunch socket, this is chopped in the same way, right to the end of the component as in Fig 108. The mortice cannot be narrower than the width of the chisel, so it follows that any whittling of the sides of the mortice to neaten it will make it oversize. Keep the chisel vertical and do not permit it to twist as this will also result in

an oversize mortice. The practice of first drilling a row of holes and then opening them up neither saves time nor produces a more accurate mortice.

Sawing tenons

The accurate sawing of tenons (Fig 119) is a vital skill. They should be sawn with confidence and should fit from the saw. To saw clear of the lines, for safety, is not recommended since whittling an overthick tenon to size is both more difficult and less accurate than sawing correctly in the first place. A 250mm (10in.) tenon or backsaw is the most commonly used for this purpose. Frame saws are used in Europe and by some workers in the USA, but they have never been popular in Britain since the manufacture of good-quality backsaws, and

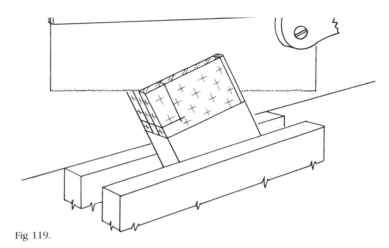

Fig 119.

20 Sawing tenon cheeks—the second stage. Do not saw to a line which is not fully in view

beginners usually find them rather clumsy.

Before starting, check over the names of the parts on Fig 95 and shade in the waste. While there is little chance of throwing away the wrong piece, it is essential that the sawdust should be removed from the waste and not from the tenon. That is, the 'kerf' (the sawcut) should be in the waste and just

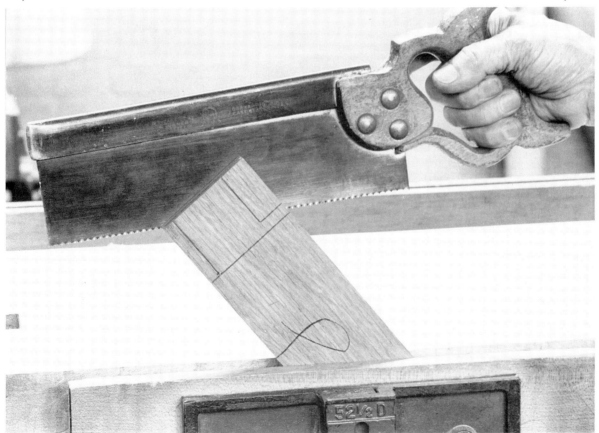

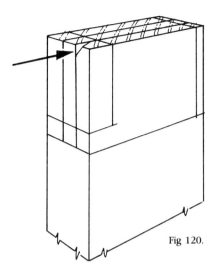

Fig 120.

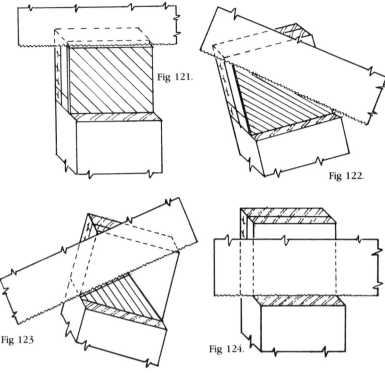

Fig 121.

Fig 122.

Fig 123

Fig 124.

Fig 125

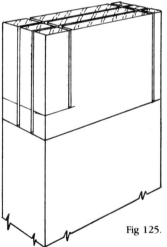

up to the line. Beginners using the thick pencil aid in Fig 105 should saw away one pencil line and leave the other intact. The technique is not difficult if the following guidelines are followed: do not saw down two gauge lines at a time; do not saw to a line which is out of sight. (A modification to the saw is described in Appendix B.)

Start sawing always at the farther corner not the nearer one. Beginners may find it useful to chisel a triangular nick there to start the saw accurately (Fig 120). With the rail held vertically in the vice, start to saw at that far corner, slowly lowering the handle until a slot is cut about 3mm ($\frac{1}{8}$in.) deep (Fig 121). Now tilt the workpiece (Fig 122) and, keeping the saw in the slot, saw from corner to corner. Then turn the work round, or stand on the other side, and saw again from corner to corner, leaving an uncut triangle in the centre (Fig 123). Now grip the work vertically and, running down the two existing sawcuts, remove this last triangle, sawing down to the knife line, but no farther.

Keep the saw horizontal (Fig 124).

If there is a set-in or haunch, saw this next. Repeat these stages on all the other tenons (Fig 125). The haunch may be sawn right off now or later.

Sawing the shoulder is most important as this is the piece left exposed. Except on wide rails, which may be planed, the shoulder should go up from the saw. Cramp to the bench, deepen the knife cut and chisel a shallow groove (Fig 126). Lay a very sharp saw in the groove and draw it back a few times to make a kerf, then saw off the cheek. Take the greatest care not to saw into the tenon (Fig 127), which would then be severely weakened. Should the waste not fall off, the cheek has probably been sawn with an arc-like motion, leaving some waste in the centre (Fig 128). Do not

saw the shoulder deeper. Prise off the waste with a chisel, then gently and carefully pare away the obstruction. Saw off the haunch if not sawn previously.

21 Trueing an over-thick tenon. A block of equal thickness has been screwed to the base of the hand router to keep it level

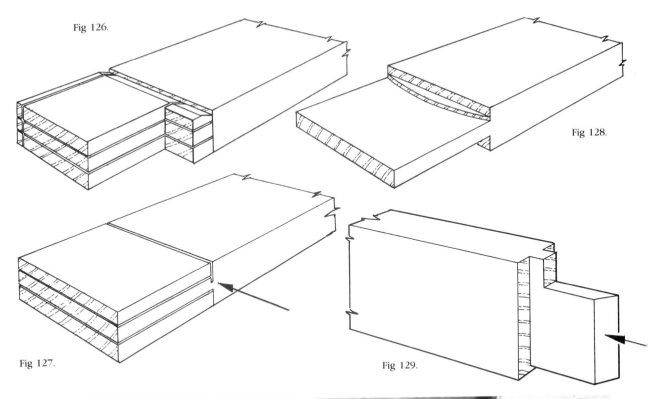

Fig 126.

Fig 128.

Fig 127.

Fig 129.

Saw off the set-in with a little to spare, and trim this back to the knife line with a chisel only just wider than the tenon size. This avoids damage to the corner of the shoulder. Finally saw the mitre (Fig 129). The tenons should be lettered or numbered to identify them with their mortices.

Make a preliminary fitting of the joints. The tenon may be too wide or too thick. Check for the latter by inserting it diagonally into the mortice (Fig 130). A tenon may be wrongly thought to be too thick when in fact it is too wide. It may have been sawn too wide or the mortice may have been chopped tapered (Fig 131), in which case trim it square. The most accurate way to correct an overthick tenon is to use a *router plane*, to the sole of which has been screwed an offcut of rail material (Fig 132).

Having checked that the tenon will enter the mortice, grip the rail in the vice and tap on the tenoned member using a woodblock and hammer (Fig 133). The hammer face is small and makes it a more precise tool than the mallet. Check every joint in this way. If the shoulder does not close, either the tenon is too long or the haunch is too long, and either of these problems can easily be corrected. But a badly sawn shoulder can only be corrected by re-squaring and taking back with a shoulder plane.

Fig 130.

Fig 132.

Fig 133.

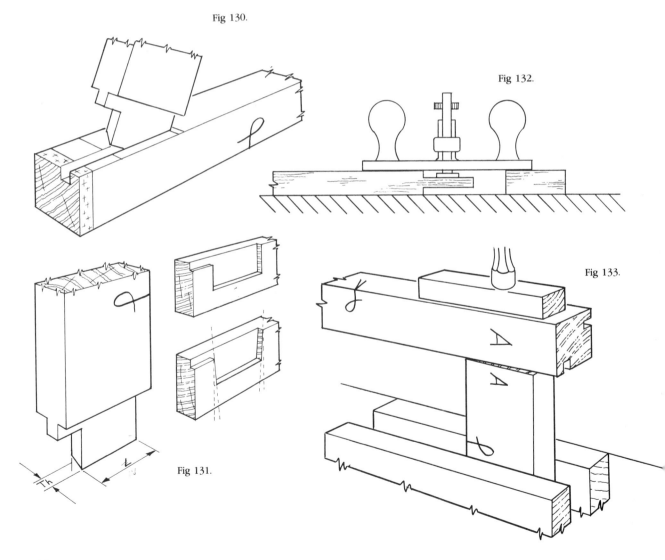

Fig 131.

Fig 134.

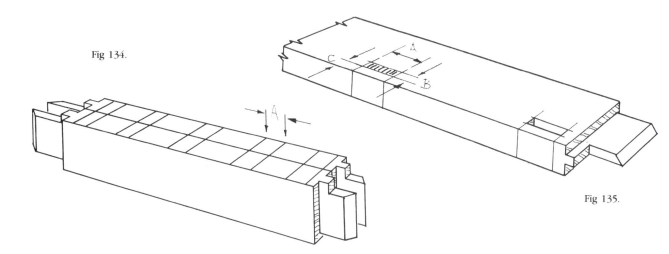

Fig 135.

Marking and chopping button mortices

Table tops are held on by *shrinkage buttons* whose making and use will be described on p.75. The mortices for these will be marked out by an experienced worker at the same time as the tenons. For simplicity these two processes have been kept separate here.

Cramp the pairs of rails together and mark the button mortice lengths on the top edge (Fig 134). The end mortices should be as close to the shoulder as is convenient. On a small table this could be just over 13mm ($\frac{1}{2}$in.), because the top needs to be held firmly at the corners. The right mortice length for a small table (*A*) is about 25mm (1in.). On larger tables there will be a proportionate increase.

Separate the rails and mark the lines a short distance down the inside face (use pencil to leave no trace later). Set a mortice gauge to the chosen chisel. Again, on small tables this could be 8mm (5/16in.) (*B*). The distance from the top edge

is the same (*C*) and so is the depth. Gauge the mortices and shade the waste (Fig 135). Then cramp the rail to the bench, and cut the mortices in the normal way. Nowadays these mortices are often cut with a power router, and the resulting round ends are quite acceptable providing that they are extra to the marked length. The common commercial practice of cutting a groove along the entire length of the rail should not be followed, because the remaining wood tends to break away. If working by hand, check that the required depth has been achieved everywhere.

It is impossible to dictate the number of mortices or their spacing, but as a rule it is better to have too many rather than too few, particularly on the end rails.

Planing tapers

Before the glue-up, the inside faces of the legs must be tapered. To do this, saw the lower end of the leg accurately to length and gauge the amount of the taper on the end grain, working from the true face and the true edge (Fig 136). Plane away the waste between the joint and this gauge mark. Check with a straightedge and a try-square. Some pencil marks near the joint line help to prevent inadvertent planing away of the fitted joint.

Short legs can be held in the

pencil marking

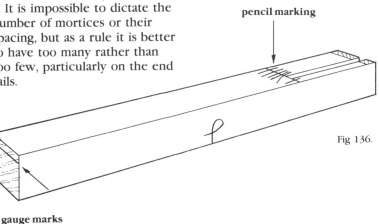

Fig 136.

gauge marks

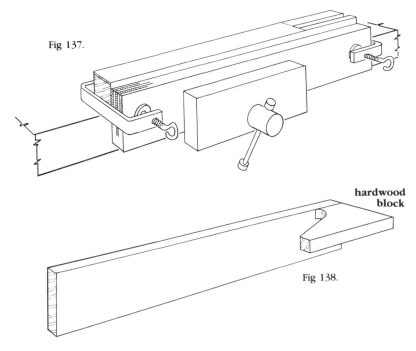

Fig 137.

hardwood
block

Fig 138.

surface.

In the case of rails, prepare the inside face and the bottom edge. A sharp, finely set smoothing plane should be used, although a difficult patch may need the scraper or scraper plane (see pp. 56 and 63). Finally, go over these surfaces with glasspaper. Soften the sharp 'arris' or corner between these two surfaces, but no other corners. Test the corner for over-sharpness by rubbing with clenched knuckles, not with the ball of the thumb which is less sensitive. Before applying the finish (see p.76), protect the tenons by wrapping them in transparent adhesive paper or masking tape. The button mortices require no such protection as there is no glueing involved.

Clean up the two inner surfaces of the legs in the same way, taking care to work only on the tapers and not to plane away the joint. Before applying a finish protect the glueing areas with tape (Fig 139). This can be put on approximately and trimmed to size with a cutting gauge and a knife. The masked-off area should be minutely smaller than the glueing area to ensure that no glue sticks to an unpolished place.

vice to plane the first surface, but then having lost parallel they can no longer be so gripped. The general method of working against a planing stop is difficult for beginners. There are three alternatives:
1. Grip the work by its ends in a sash cramp and in turn grip this in the bench vice with the leg resting on the benchtop. Flush vice jaws will require a packing piece.
2. Grip a suitable length of board or plywood in the vice and cramp the leg to it using light G-cramps or small handscrews (Fig 137).
3. Prepare a length of multi-ply or wood about 20mm ($\frac{3}{4}$in.) thick. Glue and screw to one end a notched hardwood block of about the same thickness (Fig 138). The device is gripped in the vice with the block on the benchtop. The work is simply pushed into the notch for planing.

Polishing insides
The polishing of insides and backs not only produces a superior-looking job, it has a further purpose. The wood is sealed from the atmosphere and will not so easily absorb or give out moisture, the cause of most distortion. Additionally it will be less attractive to boring insects. Polish the inside surfaces before glueing up while they are still accessible. This avoids polish building up in the corners, and excess glue can be more easily cleaned from a polished

Fig 139.

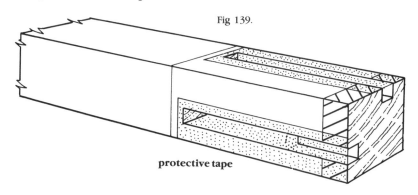

protective tape

Glueing up

Before applying any glue, make sure that all the pieces fit together correctly. Cramp together one long side rail and two legs, using a sash cramp and wood blocks (Fig 140). The blocks cannot be picked up from the waste box, they must be carefully made to the same thickness as the rail and be about as long as the width of the rail. The cramp bar must be central below the rail and the cramping blocks must be no lower than the underside of the rail (Fig 141). If the cramp bar is too high, as at *A*, the shoulders will open at *AA*. If the cramp bar is too low, as at *B*, the shoulders will open at *BB*. By looking endwise on at Fig 141 you will see that if the cramping block is low, i.e. on the bar, the leg will rotate, in this case anti-clockwise, opening at *CC*.

Make sure that the rail matches up to the length marking at the top of the leg (Fig 142). If it is too high, use a sash cramp between the rail and the leg foot to pull it into place (Fig 143). If the rail is too low, correct the position with a G-cramp and a stout block (Fig 144). A slight adjustment of the tenon or mortice may be necessary.

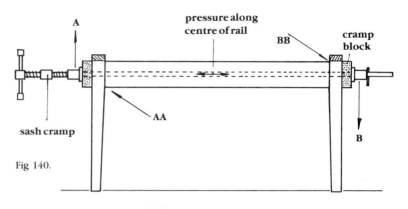

Fig 140.

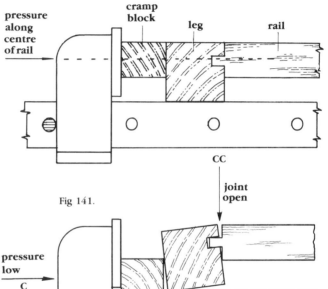

Fig 141.

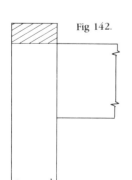

Fig 142.

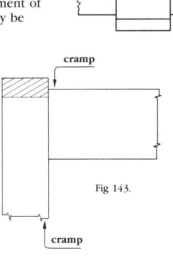

Fig 143.

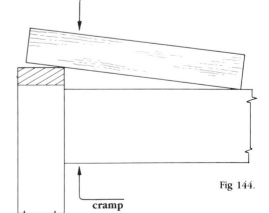

Fig 144.

22 Planing the shoulder of a tenon. Small shoulders should fit straight from the saw. On wider shoulders a shoulder plane is essential

Check that the diagonals are equal with a thin lath and pencil (Fig 145). If they are not, move the sash cramp slightly in the direction of the longer diagonal (Fig 146).

Now examine the fit of the shoulders in this position. If the fit is good, mark the identifying letter with a tick (Fig 147). If the fit is not satisfactory, mark the open point (Fig 148) and dismantle. Using a sharp knife, re-square from this point

(Fig 149). Cramp the rail to the benchtop or to a stout block held in the vice and remove the excess with a shoulder plane (see photograph 22).

When firmly cramped up with well-fitting shoulders and equal diagonals, check that the legs are not in twist using winding strips (Fig 150). Unless the mortices or tenons are very badly cut, it is usually possible to wrench the legs free of twist.

Summary
1. Is the rail in the right place?
2. Are the diagonals equal?
3. Are the shoulders a good fit?
4. Are the legs in wind?

These are the normal tests for any flat frame. Repeat this process with the other long side and the remaining legs, and when the results are satisfactory glue the pieces together.

Having glued the two long frames, put in the short rails. Before glueing, repeat all the tests with two additional ones. Test that the top diagonals are equal (Fig 151) and that there is no twist across the top of the table (Fig 152). The top diagonals can be pulled into place with a loop of cord tensioned with a twisting stick (Fig 153). Over-correct slightly to allow for springback.

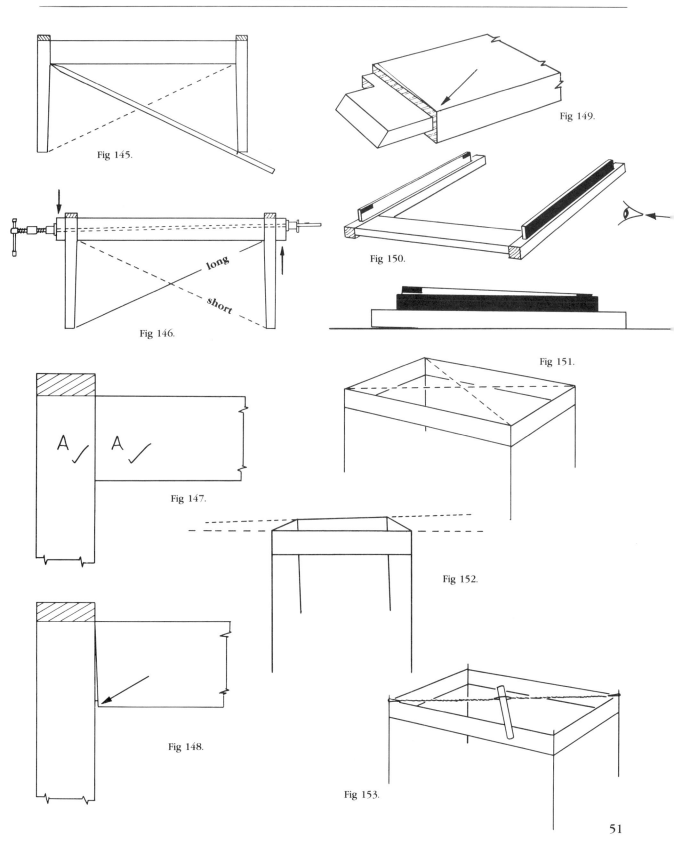

Fig 145.

Fig 146.

long

short

Fig 147.

A ✓   A ✓

Fig 148.

Fig 149.

Fig 150.

Fig 151.

Fig 152.

Fig 153.

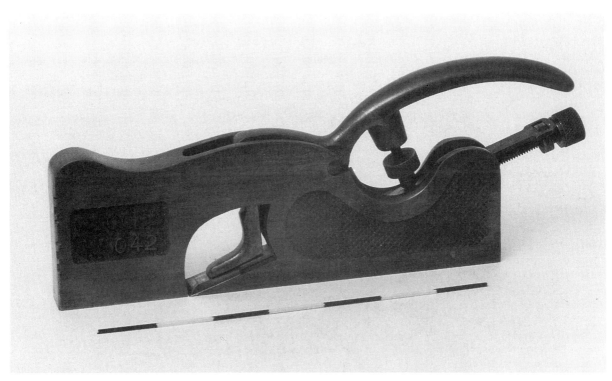

23 The Record shoulder plane. This is delightful to use and is now becoming available again.

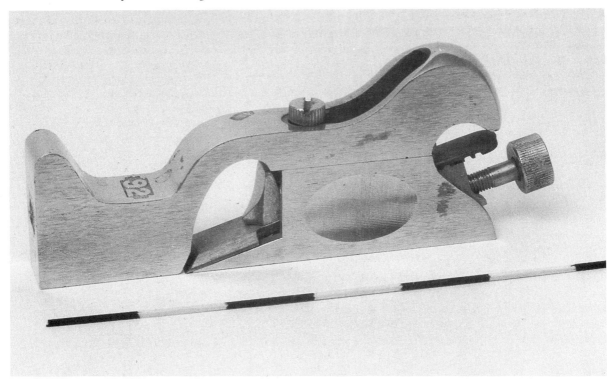

24 The small Stanley shoulder plane. An all round plane for cutting small rebates and simple mouldings (inch scale)

Types of glue

The choice of glue is important though to some extent a personal matter. Scotch (i.e. animal) glue, heated in a water-jacketed gluepot is much less used these days. It still finds favour with restorers for whom in any case it is a necessity for veneering. It is not waterproof, requires overnight hardening, and deteriorates if allowed to boil.

Synthetic resin glues are used by both individual craftsmen and industry. There are two types. The *combined hardener* type consists of a synthetic resin and a hardener, both dehydrated. When mixed with water the chemistry begins. Assembly time is about 10 minutes. Minimum cramping time is given for various temperatures. Perhaps four to six hours would be typical but overnight hardening should be given before a joint is subjected to any strain. Cascamite is at present typical of this type.

The *separate hardener* type consists of a resin and a hardener solution (generally formic acid). It is also available as a powder to be converted to resin in smaller quantities by the addition of water. Resin is applied to one half of the joint and hardener to the other. Assembly time is about the same but the minimum cramping time is rather shorter (a table of assembly and cramping times is given below). This is a very clean glue and there is no waste. Aerolite 300 is typical

Assembly			Minimum cramping		
°C	°F	Mins	°C	°F	Hrs
15	59	25	15	59	$3\frac{1}{2}$
20	68	15	20	68	$2\frac{1}{4}$
25	77	10	25	77	$1\frac{1}{2}$

(306 is the powder form). Synthetic resin glues are waterproof and mould resistant. They are 'gap filling' in that slightly loose-fitting joints will be securely held.

PVA glues (polyvinyl acetate) are nowadays probably the most widely used. There are many makes on the market and new ones are constantly appearing. They come ready mixed and are applied straight from the bottle. Some have a tendency to stain hardwoods, oak in particular, so a new brand should be tested before use. They harden quickly—two hours or even less being a minimum cramping time. However, overnight hardening is still recommended before subjecting a joint to strain. Generally these glues are not waterproof although the claim is being made for some of the newer products. PVA glues are mostly white (some are yellow) and they dry semi-transparent.

Rubber-based impact adhesives are of little use to the wood craftsman. The very expensive epoxy resins like Araldite and the 'superglues' are occasionally useful to get out of a jam but have no place in general construction.

Application

To obtain an even coating a serrated spreader is best (Fig 154). Made of plastic, they are supplied with impact glues and most hardware shops will give a few away to regular customers. Otherwise make one from an offcut of plastic laminate with a three-cornered file.

Stikibond

Fig 154.

Cleaning up the outside

Surplus glue on the inside surfaces presents no problems if the previous instructions have been followed; it can easily be flicked off. To remove surplus glue from the external surfaces, plane the glue off from all four sides, then sharpen the smoothing plane and set it finely to obtain a good finish.

The actual holding of a small table will depend greatly on the size of the individual bench. First clamp the table firmly. This can be done by threading it onto the vice using a heavy batten to hold it in place (Fig 155), and using small blocks or wedges to support the tapered legs. If this is not feasible the table can be reversed, with legs outwards (Fig 156). This will be necessary for larger tables anyway. The leg is held firm for planing by an angled prop. Plane inwards from the leg to level the joint and finish with a part-circular stroke to avoid cutting across the grain on the leg (Fig 157). Check carefully that the joint remains flat using a metal rule (Fig 158).

The horn or 'joggle' remaining on the leg should now be sawn off close; splitting out can be avoided by chiselling a small bevel just below the top of the rail (Fig 159). Then plane it level. Always plane inwards and check with a rule (Fig 160). Excess planing (Fig 161) will result in a badly fitting top. For this part of the job, use the smoothing plane as much as possible. However there is always the occasional spot which does not respond to this treatment. This can be cleaned up with the cabinet scraper (see p.56) or, better still, particularly for larger areas, with

53

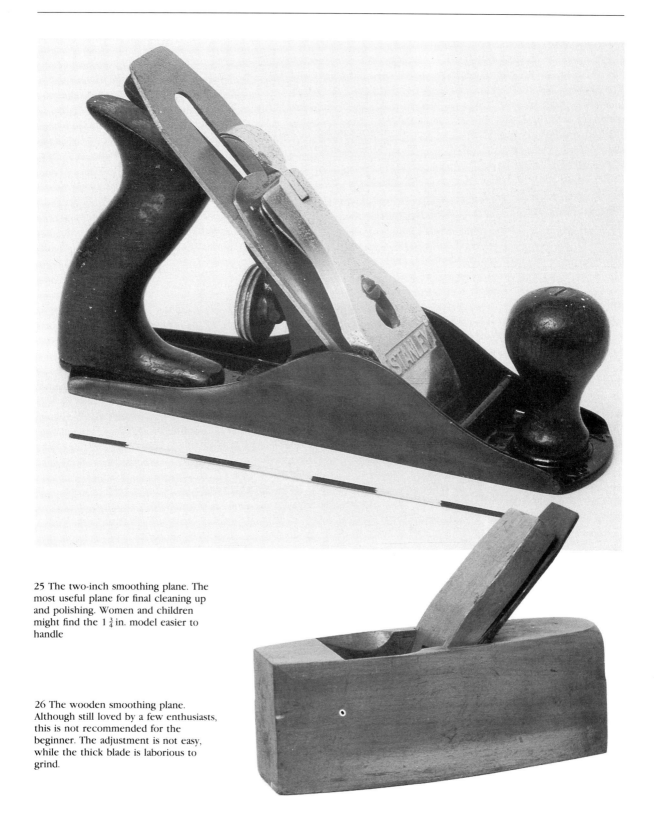

25 The two-inch smoothing plane. The most useful plane for final cleaning up and polishing. Women and children might find the $1\frac{3}{4}$ in. model easier to handle

26 The wooden smoothing plane. Although still loved by a few enthusiasts, this is not recommended for the beginner. The adjustment is not easy, while the thick blade is laborious to grind.

the scraper plane (see p.63) which ensures that the surface remains flat.

Finish by 'sanding' (i.e. glasspapering). Glasspaper comes in several grades, but a grade coarser than 80 is not necessary. Be warned, however, that glasspaper is not a cover-up for bad planing technique or for poorly sharpened scrapers. Garnet or aluminium oxide papers give better results and last longer, although these are slightly more expensive. Further information about sanding is given under 'Cleaning up the top' (p.62).

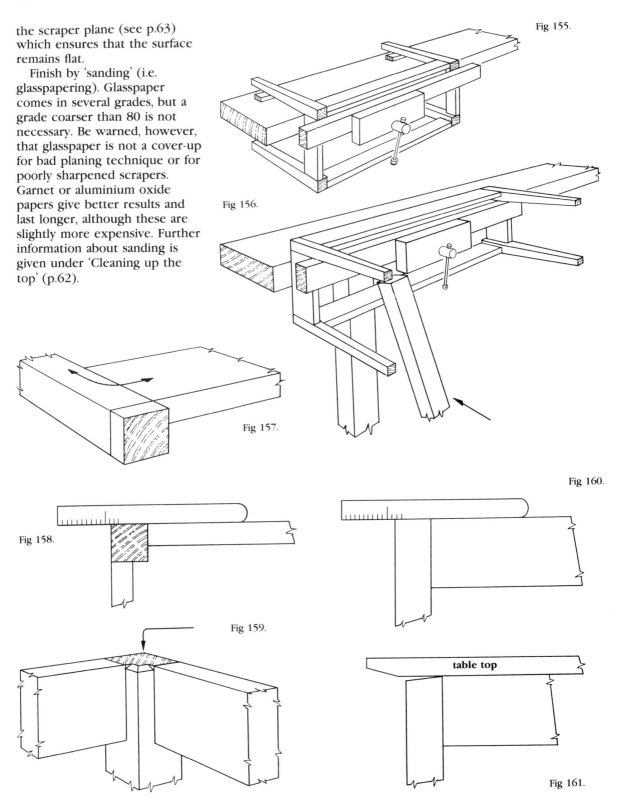

Fig 155.

Fig 156.

Fig 157.

Fig 158.

Fig 159.

Fig 160.

table top

Fig 161.

The cabinet scraper

Wood can be removed in either of two ways—by cutting or by scraping. Fig 162 shows the cleaving action of an axe. It will be seen that for the most part the cutting edge is clear of the wood. The action of the chisel and plane is somewhat similar; the wood splits ahead of the cutting edge with the result that the edge of the tool lasts a long time. But in the scraping action (Fig 163), the edge is in constant and heavy contact with the wood and blunts very quickly. In addition, cutting requires less effort than scraping, and sharpening takes less time. The scraper, having no sole like that of the plane, easily makes an accurate surface untrue, so it should only be used when you are in a jam and when you want to clean up an existing surface or shape. When choosing scraping, make sure that the tool works at its maximum efficiency. In fact, scraping is an unfortunate word because it leads people to accept a very low standard of performance.

The cabinet scraper is a rectangular piece of tempered steel varying in size between 75 × 40mm (3 × 1½in.) and 150 × 70mm (6 × 2¾in.). The most convenient size is 125 × 65mm (5 × 2½in.). Very flexible scrapers are easy to use but get very hot. A thick, rigid one stays cooler but is tiring on the fingers.

Having some specialist equipment for sharpening makes sure that the job is well done rather than a hasty touch-up. This equipment consists of a vice, a file, an oilstone and a burnisher. Fig 164 shows a set of vice jaws which not only makes the filing easier but also reduces the amount of unpleasant noise which can result. Arrange things so that when the leather linings are in place, the jaws are naturally open just a little more than the scraper's thickness.

Do not stint on the file. Buy a 250mm (10in.) or better still a 300mm (12in.) single-cut millsaw file. Put on a decent and identifiable handle, keep it in a plastic sleeve and use it exclusively for the sharpening of scrapers. When purchasing an oilstone, any fine artificial stone will serve, although my preference is for a small circular axe stone. A 75mm (3in.) Carborundum pattern is available with a fine and a medium side. A fine lubricating oil is used with this.

The last requirement is a burnisher (Fig 165). All sorts of things are pressed into service here, from the backs of gouges to ground-off files, but if the material is not hard enough, grooves will eventually be formed in it and then the finest edge will not be attainable. I recommend the purchase of an engineer's round lathe tool bit 100mm (4in.) long by 6 or 8mm (¼in. or 5/16in.) diameter, in high-speed steel. Eclipse and several other firms make these. The cost is not excessive considering that the tool will last a lifetime. Once again, make a nicely finished handle and keep the tool wrapped in a rag or in a plastic sleeve.

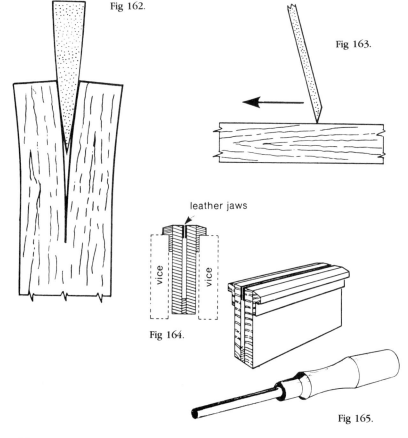

Fig 162.

Fig 163.

leather jaws

vice

vice

Fig 164.

Fig 165.

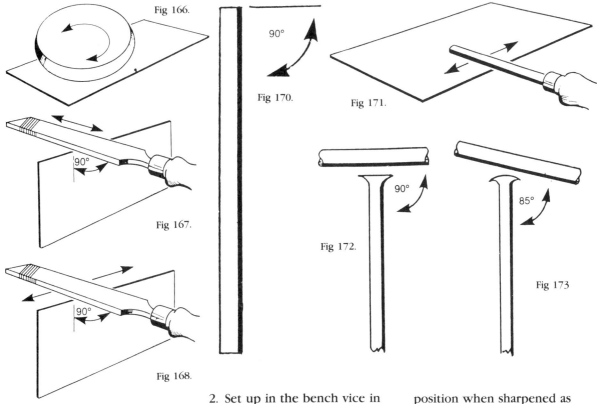

Fig 166.

Fig 167.

Fig 168.

Fig 170.

Fig 171.

Fig 172.

Fig 173

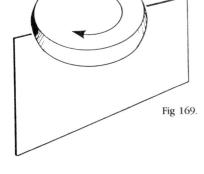

Fig 169.

Sharpening the cabinet scraper is a procedure often described, but there are several features worth pointing out. This is how it is done:

1. Stone the four edges flat, removing any burr from previous sharpenings (Fig 166).

2. Set up in the bench vice in the scraper jaws and file straight and square, removing all traces of former edges (Fig 167).
3. Finish by draw-filing, still keeping the file square to the scraper (Fig 168).
4. Repeat this with the stone to remove any file marks (Fig 169).
5. Repeat these procedures on the other long edge.
6. Remove any burr by stoning (Fig 166). There are now two long edges trued to 90° in section as in Fig 170.
7. Lightly oil the burnisher and burnish the faces flat (Fig 171).
8. Return to the special jaws and burnish the edge with a few firm strokes at exactly 90°. This produces edges in section as in Fig 172.
9. Repeat at an angle of about 85°, to produce the cutting edge in section as in Fig 173. Fig 174a shows the cutting

position when sharpened as described. In Fig 174b too much angle has been given in the burnishing with the result that the tool only cuts when held at an inconveniently low angle. In use cut with a slicing action (Fig 175c), not as in Figs 175a and b. To obtain shavings of a manageable width, bend the tool with thumb pressure. Some workers tape up their thumbs with surgical tape as protection when the scraper becomes hot. Note that the scraper should take off thin and curling shavings. If only dust is made, the tool needs sharpening. But *beware*! A flat planed surface can easily be upset by excessive use of the scraper. There is a tendency to cut away the softer parts of the timber, leaving the harder parts high. This effect becomes very obvious when the wood is polished.

Do not sand before scraping. Even the finest sanding leaves deposits of abrasive particles in the pores of the wood. Using the scraper after sanding means that its keen edge will be quickly ground off by these particles. The same applies to the cutting edges of planes.

As for re-sharpening, many claim that this can be quickly done by removing the burr, either by stoning or by burnishing, and then re-burnishing, and then normal way. The burnishing angle must be increased each time until the angle of working (Fig 174b) becomes awkward. On balance I do not think that the moments saved by avoiding making a brand new cutting edge are worth while. If the file, stone and burnisher are stored readily to hand, I feel sure most readers will want to do the job properly each time.

After a long interval, shaped scrapers are becoming available again, but it is always possible to file or grind a small scraper to any convenient curve. These shaped scrapers are also useful for faceplate work on the lathe (stationary, of course, for example when removing circular marks from the inside of a bowl). Preferably the faceplate should be removed from the lathe and held in the vice.

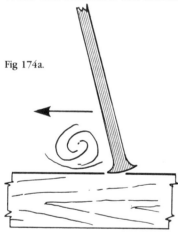

Fig 174a.

Fig 174b.

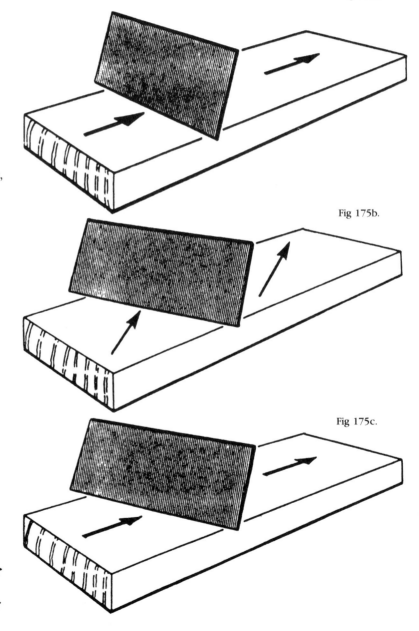

Fig 175a.

Fig 175b.

Fig 175c.

Jointing the top

The first aim is to get the most pleasing appearance. Sort the boards about to find the best result and the most inconspicuous joints. At the same time bear in mind that all the boards should plane on the same direction. In order to achieve the best visual effect this is not always possible, nevertheless it should always be aimed at.

In order to keep warping of the finished table top to a minimum, the heart side of alternate boards should generally be uppermost (Fig 176). However, when initially selecting for a top, boards should be chosen as close to radial in the log as possible, i.e. with annual rings at right angles to the face (Fig 177). This is described in the textbooks as 'quarter sawn'.

There are three approaches to jointing so individual circumstances come into account. Boards can be jointed in the rough and planed level and to thickness later. This method gives the maximum thickness. A slight preliminary skimming can be given in order to see the colour and grain pattern for matching. The boards can be thicknessed, generally by hand, to slightly oversize, then jointed and

27 The try or trying plane—its considerable length ensures accuracy when planing long edge joints

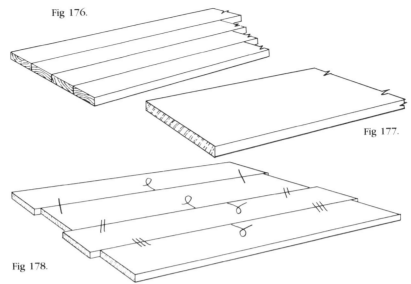

Fig 176.

Fig 177.

Fig 178.

cleaned up. This is the way most workers without machines operate. With a planer-thicknesser, or with preplaned, bought-in material, the boards are carefully jointed in the finished thickness, when very little subsequent cleaning up should be necessary. Warped wide boards will require cutting down the middle and re-jointing. Boards may also need cutting in width to suit smaller machinery, for example, a 150mm (6in.) planer or thicknesser. This is not so detrimental as it may appear since a large proportion of wide boards offered for sale are warped to some extent.

Having decided on the layout of the boards, check them for twist with the winding strips, mark the best-looking side with

the face mark and identify the joints (Fig 178). The joints can now be planed either by hand or on a surface planer.

Working by hand, a try-plane or joiner is the correct tool to use. Joints of moderate length can be made with a finely set jack plane. The cutter should be ground absolutely square since the corners will not be used. It is quite useful to have two cutters for the try-plane, one all square, for jointing, and one with the corners rounded and the very slightest of curves, for surface work (Fig 179).

Fig 179.

As in the early planing exercises, plane right through to clean the edge then if you are a beginner mark each end with a pencil and, with the finest of cuts, plane avoiding the extreme ends until no further shavings will appear. Use the edge grip throughout. Check continually with a try-square. Then plane from end to end until the first full-length, full-width shaving is obtained. Stop at once and repeat on the matching board. The joint can now be tested.

Grip one board in the vice and stand its partner on it for examination. Gently poke one side at the corner. If it pivots (Fig 180), it is high in the middle and a shaving needs to be removed. If the top board does not pivot but falls off, either the joint is good or it is hollow in the centre. Careful inspection will ascertain which. On a long joint, say over 1m (3ft.), a very slight hollow is acceptable. On shorter joints perfection should be aimed at.

Now test the joint for flatness with a straightedge (Fig 181). If any correction is necessary, using the all-square cutter, make a very slight adjustment to the lateral lever and test, shaving by shaving. Be careful when correcting in this way not to upset the joint lengthways. Needless to say, full-width shavings must be produced every time. When both tests have been passed the joint is ready to glue, but before doing so conduct a dry run with all the cramps in place. Check that the cramps themselves are on a flat surface.

In the days of scotch glue the joint was simply 'rubbed' and left to harden. This technique is not applicable to the modern

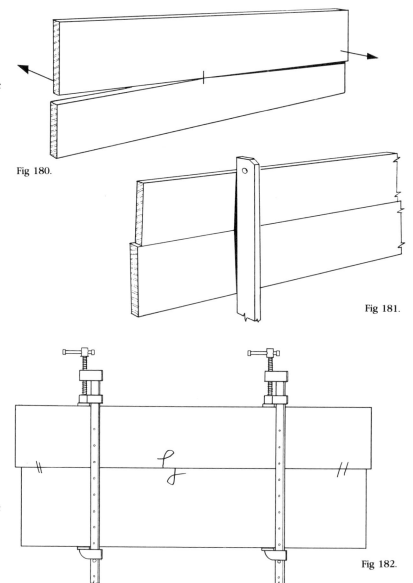

Fig 180.

Fig 181.

Fig 182.

glues which will require sash cramps or a substitute (Fig 182). Ideally one joint at a time should be glued but often, to save time, two or three boards are glued at once. Lay a strip of paper between the work and the cramp bar to prevent glue-iron staining. Make sure that the boards lie flat on the cramp bars; if necessary pull them down into place with a G-

cramp. Any slight steps on the surface can be knocked down by the use of a block below which is slightly thicker than the height of the cramp bar (Figs 183 and 184). It is worth keeping a special hardwood block for this purpose. When more than two sash cramps are employed, they should be spaced on opposite sides of the table top, which helps to

60

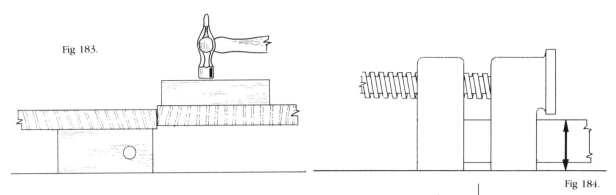

Fig 183.

Fig 184.

prevent bowing.

Jointing by machine on a surface planer broadly follows the same pattern. Having established the layout of the boards with the true faces up, alternate sides are marked with a distinguishing mark (Fig 185). When jointing, this face must run against the fence of the planer. In this way an error in squareness between the fence and the planer table is corrected, i.e. measuring from the true faces one board will be planed at say 89° and the other at 91°. Although the error may be very small, in a top of four pieces it is incorporated six times. This can result in an appreciable bow when the top is glued up.

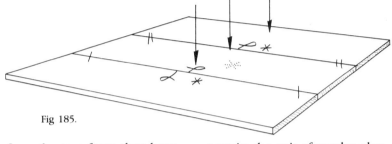

Fig 185.

Dowelling the edge joints

An edge joint is sometimes dowelled. This is done not so much to strengthen the joint since modern glues are adequate, but rather to ensure a good line-up where a board has a bend in it or to facilitate the glueing up of a number of boards at one go. The traditional method is shown in Figs 186 and 187.

Cramp the boards together and square across at intervals. Separate and gauge the centres from the true faces then bore, using either a dowelling bit or brad point drill; an engineer's twist drill with no point will not start accurately enough. Avoid buying machine dowelling bits with a screw nose, they pull in far too rapidly with almost total loss of control. Countersink the holes slightly to leave space for any slight whiskers round the hole and for exuded glue. The dowels should be a little shorter than the combined depths of the two holes. Their ends are slightly chamfered (a touch with a pencil sharpener will do this). A shallow sawn groove

permits the exit of surplus glue (Fig 188). Where a number of dowels is to be prepared, a simple jig (Fig 189) speeds up the process.

Alternatively one of the commercial dowelling tools can be used or else dowel marker pins (Fig 190). When using the latter, drill a series of holes in one piece where convenient, (no particular marking out is required), then insert the dowel marker pins. Lay both boards on a flat surface, cramping one if possible, then bring them together and either tap with a hammer or lightly cramp

28 Dowel bits. (*Top*) The conventional dowel bit with square shank to fit the brace. (*Bottom*) The brad point or lip and spur type, designed for an electric drill

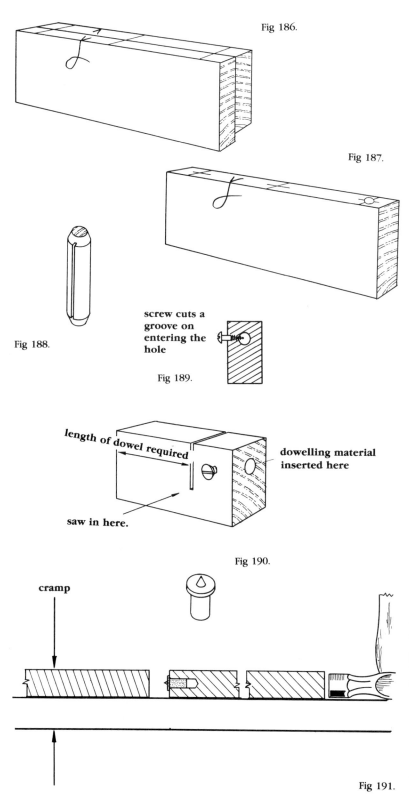

Fig 186.

Fig 187.

Fig 188.

screw cuts a groove on entering the hole

Fig 189.

length of dowel required

dowelling material inserted here

saw in here.

Fig 190.

cramp

Fig 191.

(Fig 191). Drill the holes in the second board where the centres have marked it. Reinforcing with loose tongues and using modern glues is no improvement on this method, and is a process generally reserved for securing lippings to man-made boards.

Cleaning up the top

When the glue is completely dry the surfaces can be levelled. Use a try-plane with a slightly curved blade or a jack plane. First work diagonally across the grain (Fig 192) and finally lengthwise (Fig 193). Try to avoid working too much at the edges. Test the true face with a straightedge and long winding strips, then gauge and plane to thickness. A very finely set smoothing plane should compete the surfacing. Inspect by looking along the top into the light. On a thinnish top small local blemishes can be planed out by piling a handful of shavings beneath the offending area and using great pressure.

The cabinet scraper (see p.56) can finish off the job but the scraper plane (see p.63) is better because, having a sole, it will not produce hollows. On difficult material, particularly tropical woods with interlocking grain, it is sometimes advisable to sharpen up, set the cut and cap iron very fine, and plane across the grain throughout, finishing along the grain with a freshly sharpened scraper plane.

The finishing will be completed by sanding. The most useful are garnet and aluminous oxide papers which have a longer life than common glasspaper. For preparatory sanding use 80 grit. This is

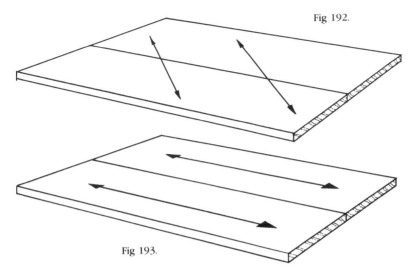

Fig 192.

Fig 193.

using either an oilstone, an oilstone slip, an axestone or a dead smooth file (Fig 194). File or grind the edge to an angle of 45° (Fig 195). This angle is important, a very slight curve is not detrimental but a hollow edge must definitely be avoided. Again rub off the burr on the flat side.

Sharpen the edge in the manner of a plane iron (see p.8), but at 45° thus removing any file marks. The sharp corners can be rounded slightly. This edge must be very keen and there must be no trace of a bevel on the flat side. A wooden holder similar to a spokeshave blade holder (Fig 196) may be a help. Be sure that no burr remains on the flat side. With the blade flat on the bench, bevel down, burnish the flat

usually enough for coarse grained woods such as oak, elm and teak, but for more closely grained woods, such as the mahogany families, use 120 grit afterwards. Veneered work incorporating mitres or inlays will require 180 grit, which is fine enough to permit a circular motion over those parts. The very finest work and the polishing process require 240 grit. Orbital sanders will stand one grade coarser at all the stages (e.g. 60 followed by 100 then 150).

Hand sand along the grain using a cork sanding block. Avoid rounding over the edges excessively. Likewise avoid aggressively sharp corners which damage easily. The test for this sharpness is to rub the edge with clenched knuckles (not the ball of the thumb). Before commencing the actual polishing wipe over the work with a 'tacky cloth'.

The scraper plane

The scraper plane, which removes fine shavings, will produce a good finish on all hardwoods. It is particularly

useful on tropical woods with their difficult interlocking grain. Softwoods do not respond well to scraping.

Sharpen the blade, remove all previous burr from the flat side,

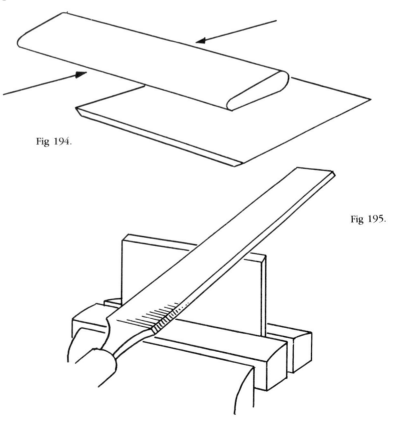

Fig 194.

Fig 195.

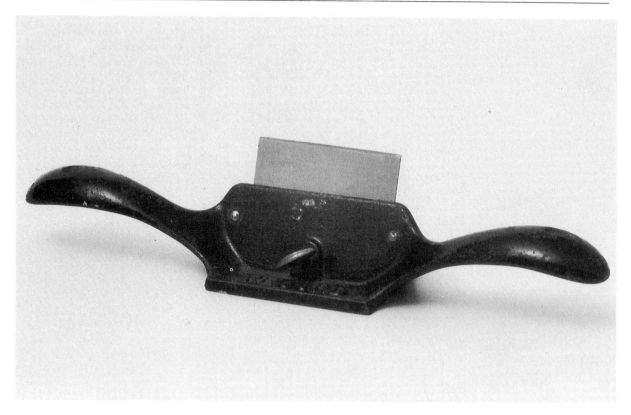

29 The scraper plane for cleaning up difficult woods before polishing. It is particularly valuable on tropical timbers with interlocking grains

face for about 20 to 30 strokes using firm pressure and a drop of oil. The burnisher must remain absolutely flat (Fig 197).

Grip the blade in a vice, bevel side to the sharpener, and with a slightly oiled burnisher begin to burnish firmly at 45°. Slowly raise the handle until the burnisher makes an angle of 15° to the horizontal (i.e. 75° to the blade). About 30 to 40 strokes will be needed according to the pressure applied (Figs 198, 199 and 200). The edge will now have a definite burr or hook

(Fig 201). Repeat the process on the other edge of the blade.

To set up the plane, place the sole on a flat surface and slacken the three screws. Insert the blade with the burred side facing forward, i.e. towards the two clamping screws, and the bevel towards the single adjusting screw and the operator. With the blade resting on the flat surface, tighten up the clamping screws. Keep the single adjusting screw slack. The scraper may cut now, producing a fine shaving. If it does not, take up the slack on the adjusting screw then give the finest turn. The more this screw is tightened, the coarser will be the cut. The more the blade is

bent, the narrower will be the shaving. Naturally the best surface will be produced from a light cut.

When using the scraper plane, as with all planes, slightly lubricate the sole. Work along the grain but with the blade held diagonally (Fig 202). Long, wide, thin, silky shavings should be produced. When only dust is produced either the blade is blunt or it has been badly sharpened. Should a chatter develop through lack of pressure, resulting in ripples on the wood, change the angle of planing immediately and work over them with very firm pressure.

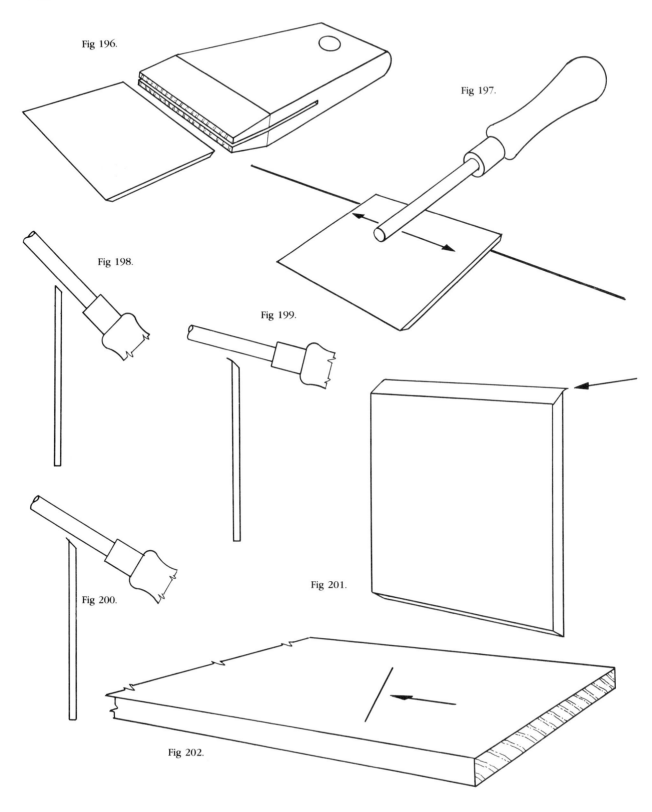

Fig 196.

Fig 197.

Fig 198.

Fig 199.

Fig 200.

Fig 201.

Fig 202.

Shaping the table top

The rectangular shape of the top (Fig 203a) shown on the basic planning in Chapter 14, can be modified to give a number of simple but more interesting shapes. The ends may be curved (b), but this must not be overdone. The long sides may be curved (c), here a very subtle curve should be aimed at. A combination of these (d) gives a less aggressive corner than the plain rectangle at (a). The corners may be rounded on (b) to give the softer shape of (e). Shape (c) can be similarly treated. All sides curved with rounded corners is shown at (f). The quarter round and the 45° cut off are both crude and to be avoided (g and h).

The drawing of these gentle curves is shown in Fig 204. A thin, flexible lath is needed of an even thickness and with straight grain. Knots and irregularities will not allow a smooth curve. Two thin pins are driven in at the ends of the proposed curve and a small pointed block is cramped on at the centre. This is gently adjusted until the required curve is found. Mark this clearly with a thin ballpoint pen. Many people object to the use of these in woodwork, but they do give a clear, even line which can be cleaned off later.

To saw out the shape, a small bandsaw is the quickest method, although many readers will no doubt use a portable jigsaw. Gentle curves can also be sawn with a handsaw, leaving the sharper curves for the bowsaw or the coping saw. Careful sawing of course reduces the amount of cleaning up later, which in most cases will be done with the metal spokeshave. The spokeshave is sharpened in the same manner as the plane (p.8). Its short blade is most conveniently handled in a simple wooden holder.

The round-faced spokeshave works concave shapes (Fig 206a) while on convex shapes the flat-faced version is employed (Fig 206b). Both shapes can be made much more accurately with the circular plane (Fig 206c). This has a sole which is adjusted to the curve. However it is a very expensive tool and at the time of writing its continued production is in some doubt.

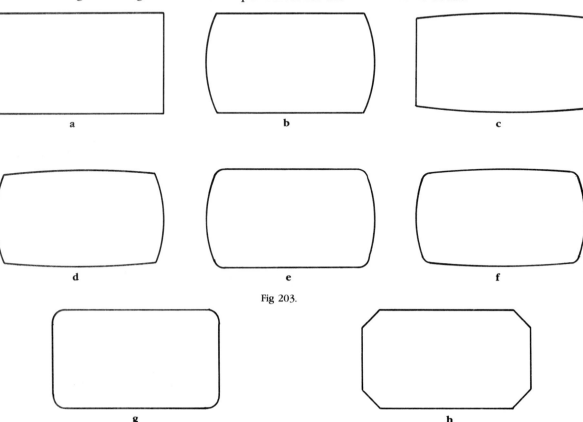

a

b

c

d

e

f

Fig 203.

g

h

30 The iron spokeshaves. Despite its lack of adjusting mechanism, the small straight-handled model is extremely pleasant to use. Wooden ones are virtually extinct now

31 The spokeshave faces. (*Top*) Flat face for convex curves. (*Bottom*) Round face for concave curves

67

32 The adjustable compass plane (or circular plane) —useful for only gradual curves

In view of the spokeshave's very short sole, a careful watch must constantly be kept on the line to make sure of obtaining a smooth curve. Also check frequently with a try-square. The direction of cutting (Fig 207) is away from the middle on the long sides and towards the middle on the end grain.

Any but the smallest tops can be held firmly by means of a small angle block (Fig 208). Fig 209 shows a table top positioned at a comfortable working height, held at one end in the bench vice and at the other by an angle block, which is cramped both to the bench and to the job.

Fig 204.

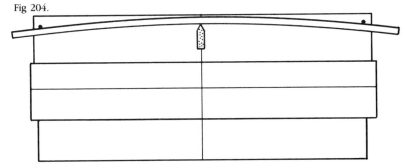

Fig 205.

Fig 206.

Fig 207.

Fig 208.

Fig 209.

cramp

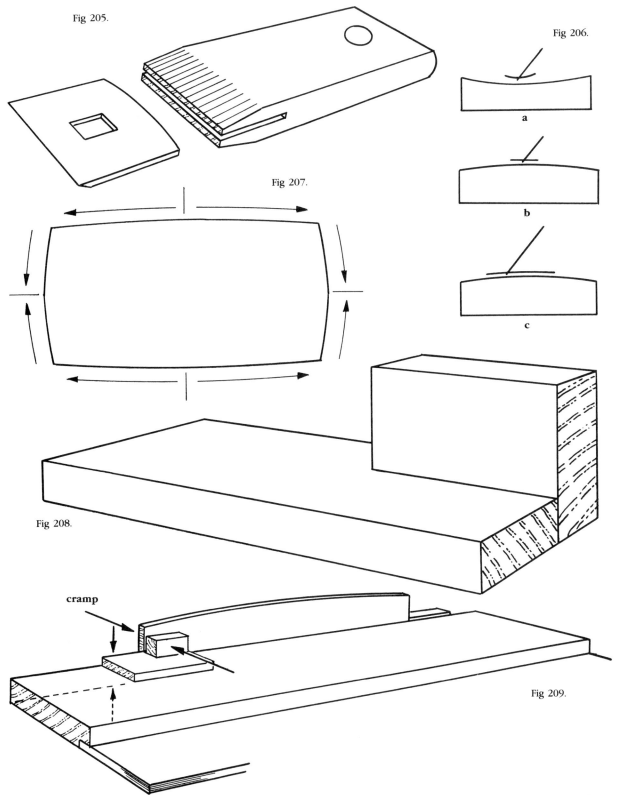

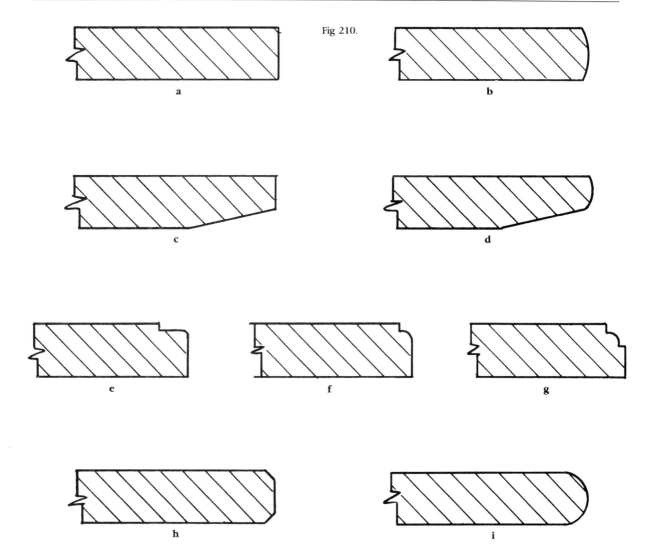

Fig 210.

Edge shaping

The edges can be left square with the sharp corner or 'arris' softened (Fig 210*a*). They may be shaped to the arc of a larger circle as *b*. A complete half round, *i*, is rather crude and not generally so successful. As with *b*, it has little to recommend it. A lighter appearance is gained when the edge is undercut, *c*. Beware of undercutting into the

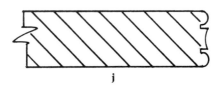

area to which the framework is attached. This edge again may be rounded, *d*. These roundings can be successfully worked with a sharp block plane followed by a glasspaper block.

The power router gives a variety of edge shapes of which *e, f,* and *g* are examples. These are only limited by the cutters or combinations of cutters available. Most of these and individually designed shapes, such as *j*, can be executed using the scratch tool. This tool is not offered for sale and must be made.

The scratch tool

Although the name might suggest a rather inferior performance this is a tool capable of producing work of accuracy and quality. In earlier times it was the main source of fine mouldings. There are several types of scratch tool. The simplest and most commonly made form is Fig. 211. Fig 212 shows a more sophisticated model which is easier to adjust and generally nicer to use. A scratch tool can also be made from two marking gauges (Figs 213 and 214). Only the stem need be made, the two fences being borrowed for the occasion. This form is particularly suitable for working on edges where the single fence models can sometimes slip sideways and damage the work.

Blades can be made from a variety of materials, for example cabinet scrapers, old handsaws and old power hacksaw blades (but not the hard cutting edge).

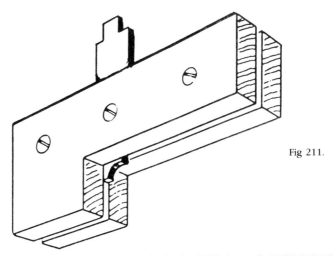

Fig 211.

33 Simple conventional scratch tool (inch scale)

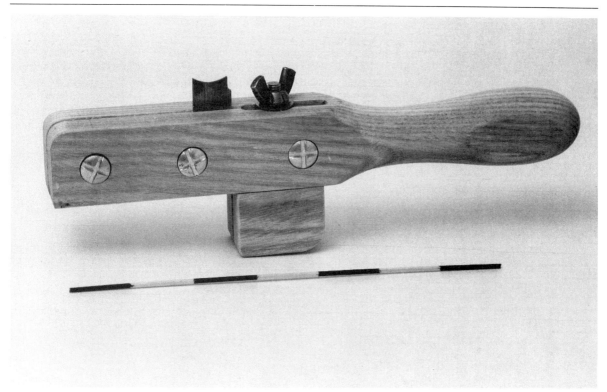

34 Improved scratch tool—it is easier to make slight adjustments by moving the fence than by upsetting the cutter (inch scale)

35 Easily made double fence scratch tool. The cutter cannot slip so it is useful for edges

Ordinary hacksaws are too thin. Thin steel sold as 'ground flat stock' can be bought for the job.

File the blades to shape, filing the cutting edge square so that the tool can be worked in both directions. After shaping, harden the blades by heating them until bright red then quenching them in oil or water. Clean up one face with emery cloth and, when bright, re-heat, preferably supported on a larger piece of metal to slow down the process. Watch the metal change colour, and when it goes light brown, quench again. This will give an edge hard enough to retain its sharpness yet which can still be sharpened by filing. The lighter the colour the harder the metal will become, and conversely too dark a colour will produce a soft tool. If the metal changes colour too quickly and you can't quench it in time, start the process afresh.

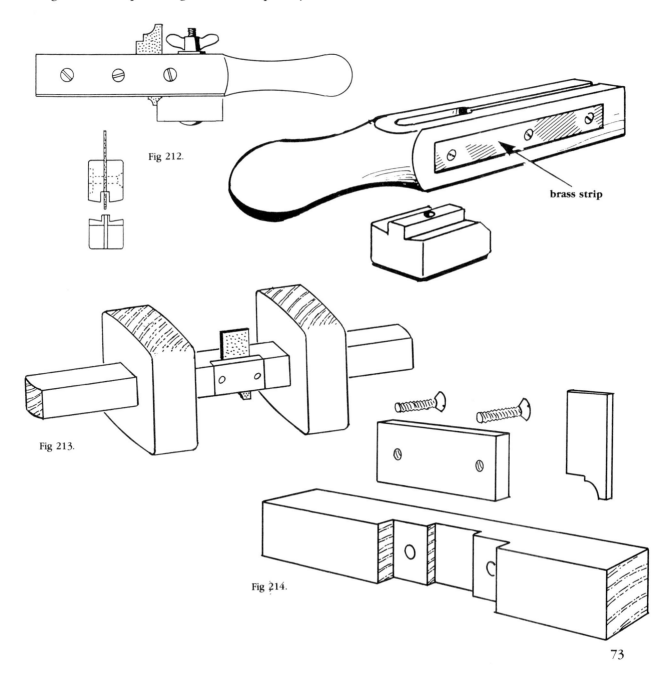

Fig 212.

brass strip

Fig 213.

Fig 214.

73

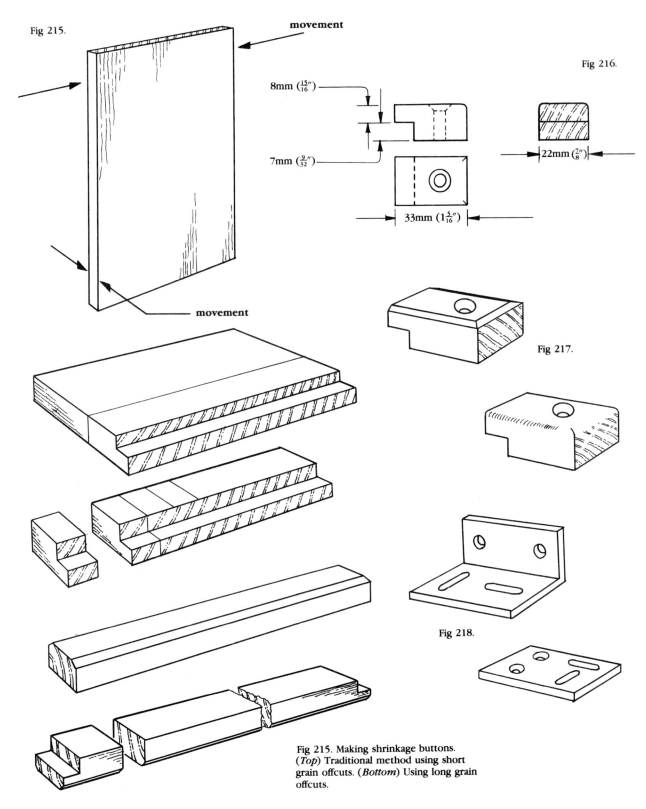

Fig 215.

movement

movement

Fig 216.

8mm ($\frac{15}{16}''$)

7mm ($\frac{9}{32}''$)

22mm ($\frac{7}{8}''$)

33mm ($1\frac{5}{16}''$)

Fig 217.

Fig 218.

Fig 215. Making shrinkage buttons. (*Top*) Traditional method using short grain offcuts. (*Bottom*) Using long grain offcuts.

Shrinkage buttons

Wood is porous and, depending on the atmosphere, will absorb or give out moisture causing it to expand or contract (Fig 215). This cannot be prevented, and allowance must be made for this movement in the construction of the table top. The amount of movement in length is negligible.

If the top is screwed directly to the frame it will either split due to contraction or bow due to expansion. This is the most common cause of split table tops. The problem is overcome using shrinkage buttons to secure the top. The mortices for these were discussed on p.47. Buttons on the long sides must have room to move in and out so their mortices need to be only slightly longer than the buttons. Buttons on the short sides or ends need room to move sideways in the mortices which must therefore be longer.

To make the shrinkage buttons there are two possible methods. The traditional method is to use short grain offcuts. Produce to thickness

and remove a rebate. Then saw off the button. Repeat the process as required.

Using the more common long grain offcuts is the second method. Produce to width and thickness, bevel or round corners, saw out a rebate and then saw off the button.

Having made the required number of buttons, lay the table top flat and cramp the frame onto it. Check that the overlap on all four sides is correct. Make an improvised depth gauge and carefully drill into the table top. The thickness of the buttons should be such that, when withdrawn sharply from the mortice, they will snap down against the table top. In other words, the length X on the button must be very slightly less than the length Y on the rail in order to obtain the vice-like grip (Fig 219).

The method of fixing is shown in Fig 220.

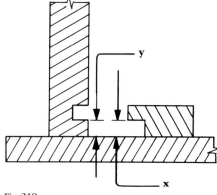

Fig 219.

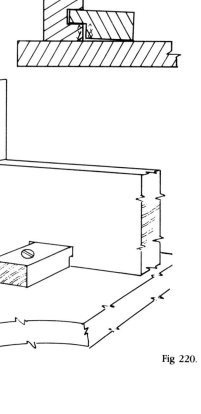

Fig 220.

Finishes

There are a number of types of finish possible on hand made woodwork, and the first that usually springs to mind is french polishing. However, not only is considerable experience necessary for this, but so is a dust-free workshop with plenty of space and good lighting. Readers wishing to become adept at this skill will have to study technical publications specifically on the subject. Apart from reproduction and restoration work, the majority of present day handmade furniture is not french polished.

Wax polishing

Wax polishing is the most common and easiest finish on handmade woodwork. It is the oldest and generally thought to be the most beautiful of the finishes. As the wax goes into the wood rather than just staying on the surface, a deep lustrous patina is achieved. A restrained semi-matt finish is quickly obtained which is enhanced further by polishing. Unfortunately a wax finish has little resistance to heat or liquids, making it unsuitable for such items as table tops, trays and possibly chair arms.

After preliminary sanding down the grades (see p.62), it is customary to apply a thin coat of sanding sealer, either cellulose-based or shellac. The latter is the more popular and easier to obtain in small quantities. If unavailable, a sealer can be made by diluting white french polish with an equal volume of methylated spirit. Avoid the vivid orange-coloured 'button polish'. Sealer is applied with a soft brush, preferably a camel hair mop. Its purpose is to fill the grain and reduce the absorption of wax in the first stages. When dry, it is rubbed down with 'flour' grade glasspaper, or the finest wet and dry paper.

A pure beeswax polish must be used. Polishes of paraffin wax and those containing silicones will no doubt be used later by the house-proud owner but these are quite unsuitable for the early coats on raw wood. A polish can be made up by shredding and dissolving 0.45kg (1lb) of pure beeswax in 280ml ($\frac{1}{2}$pt) of pure turpentine (not white spirit). This is warmed in a double boiler (i.e. a water jacket) until it becomes a soft paste. If it is too stiff, thin with more turpentine. Apply to the wood with a soft, non-fluffy rag, rubbing it well into the grain. Allow it to harden for a while and finally buff with soft dry rags. If a firm stroke across the surface with one finger leaves a mark, more rubbing is required.

Oil finishes

Oil finishing was very popular in earlier times when servant girls were cheap to give the frequent rubbings needed to maintain and improve the surface. It takes a long time and persistence to obtain a good finish, but a great advantage of an oil finish is that it can very easily be renewed.

Linseed oil is now marketed pre-packed by the decorating firms. The addition of about 10 per cent of white spirit will hasten the drying. Each application must be well rubbed in and allowed to dry for at least 24 hours. It is then rubbed down with flour grade paper, dusted off and buffed vigorously with clean rag. Further coats are applied in the same way. Several days, possibly a week, are recommended between coats. A long process but producing a rich and durable finish which is particularly suitable for bar counters and dining tables.

There are now on the market variants such as Danish oil and teak oil which shorten the process considerably. They produce a matt finish not to be compared with that of the traditional waxing method.

Wooden kitchenware can be treated by oiling with medicinal liquid paraffin; some workers recommend salad oil. Such items should be cleaned with plain water, not hot water and detergents. They benefit from regular oiling.

Polyurethane varnishing

Polyurethane varnishes are a great boon to the amateur and the small hand craftsman. They are easily applied and have great resistance to heat, liquids and abrasion. Finishes are gloss, semi-matt (or eggshell) and matt. Many brands are now available, but some are better than others, so when they discover a good one readers are advised to stick with it.

Apply the varnish with a clean soft brush, which should be kept specifically for the job, cleaned well after use and kept wrapped in kitchen film to avoid dust particles. The first coat on bare wood should be thinned slightly to about one in five. Three coats are generally recommended; the brushmarks disappear during drying. The disadvantage of the polyurethanes is their long drying time, about six hours, during which time dust can settle creating 'nibs'.

For the best finish and more

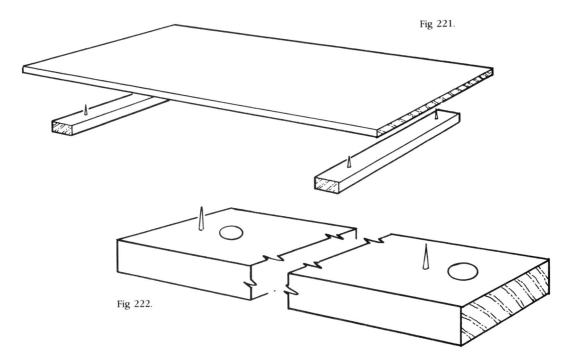

Fig 221.

Fig 222.

rapid drying the following method is recommended. After careful sanding the first thinned coat is applied, either by brush or by rubber. Rub down when thoroughly dry to remove the nibs, using wet and dry paper of at least grade 320, finer if obtainable. This sanding is generally done with the fingers. A cork block will tend only to sand on its corners, although a good job can be done by making a wood block of the same size as the cork block and glueing to it a piece of pile carpet. This has sufficient 'give' to sand over its whole area. To clean the paper and to obviate the fine powder produced by dry sanding, spray the surface with the finest mist of white spirit, using a small garden spray.

Apply further varnish with a pad of cloth (this can be stuffed with cotton wool). Start with only a small quantity of varnish, rubbing it in vigorously and

finishing along the grain. Stop when the rubber begins to drag. Using this method the varnish is touch dry quite quickly, permitting the application of several coats in a day. As a general rule, give three coats to the backs and insides and five to the tops and outsides. Always rub down carefully and wipe off between coats.

Lacquers
Cellulose lacquers should be avoided by the beginner. If applied by brush they dry too quickly and the brushmarks do not disappear, while spraying calls for expensive equipment and ideally a special workshop for that purpose.

Painting
Good painted finishes permit no short cuts. Good-quality paint and first-class preparation are the rule. Clean brushes are essential; a great proportion of the nibs on paintwork

comes from dirty brushes.

Prepare the surface to the same standard as for a polished finish. Sand down the grades and apply a coat of primer. Leave overnight, then sand off the nibs and apply the undercoat on the following day. Again, leave overnight and sand again, then give the surface two coats of gloss. In view of the long drying time for paint, work in an atmosphere as dust-free as possible, and when the job is finished close the doors and windows to prevent dust-carrying draughts. Brushes should be cleaned thoroughly at once and stored wrapped.

Components such as panels to be polished on both sides can be turned over and supported on painting sticks (Figs 221 and 222). This removes the need for two drying times. The holes permit the sticks to be tied together safely for storage.

Levelling the feet

In spite of one's best efforts, once its top has been fixed a table may still wobble on a flat surface and the feet will have to be levelled. Resist the temptation to trim the legs before the top is fixed. A slight warp on the top may be pulled down by the frame but at the cost of slightly distorting it.

Set up the complete table on a truly flat surface. The table of a largish circular saw is ideal, but a piece of thick chipboard or blockboard can be used.

Support the table and check with winding strips. Put small wedges under the feet where necessary to stop the wobble. Check that the height of the table at each corner is the same, correcting where necessary by moving the wedges.

With a small parallel block and a marking knife (Fig 223), scribe one line across the bottom of each leg. Using a try-square, carry this knifeline onto the other three faces of the leg and saw off. Aim for minimum waste, yet there should also be

sufficient to be able to saw with a fine tenon saw. After sawing, a very small bevel is cut round each foot (Fig 224). This is to prevent a sharp corner catching in a carpet thread and splitting off.

As an alternative to the knife and block, a small scriber can be made for this purpose (Fig 225). It consists merely of a rectangular block fitted with a sharp pin. With a little thought it is possible to find a location for the pin which will give four different scribing heights.

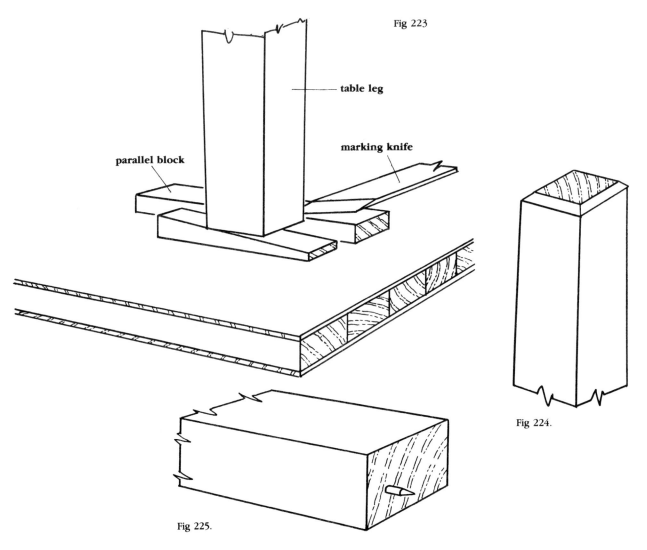

Fig 223

table leg

marking knife

parallel block

Fig 224.

Fig 225.

3 MAKING A CARCASE

Construction and design

A carcase is a box-like construction made basically from planks, in contrast to the mortice and tenon construction of posts and rails. Small cabinets, cupboards, bookshelves, wardrobes and chests of drawers are all examples of carcases. The main requirement in anything but a nailed-together job is some form of corner jointing, which will be considered later.

A carcase does not generally stand on the floor (Fig 226) and the sides may be extended to form feet (Fig 227). A box plinth is often used (Fig 228) which may be inset or out-standing. Very common is a low stool (Fig 229) following the table construction and chunky oak pieces can look well on heavy

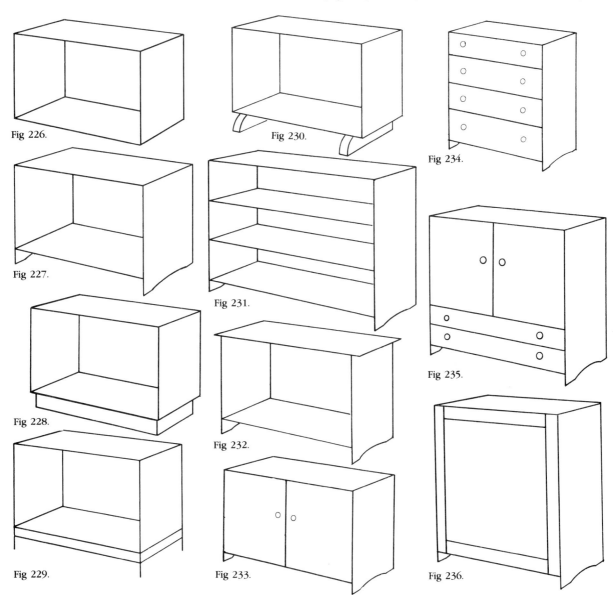

Fig 226.

Fig 230.

Fig 234.

Fig 227.

Fig 231.

Fig 235.

Fig 228.

Fig 232.

Fig 229.

Fig 233.

Fig 236.

block feet (Fig 230). Corner joints can be avoided by extending the sides (Fig 231) or by overhanging the top (Fig 232). Shelves, either fixed or movable, are generally required and often have vertical divisions. Doors, drawers or a combination of both (Figs 233, 234 and 235) complete the range of possibilities. Backs of some form, from quite elaborate constructions to plywood sheet, are normally the rule (Fig 236). Figs 227–30 require some form of dovetailing in their corner joints. Figs 231–2 avoid this joint, substituting instead a form of mortice and tenon or a dowelled joint.

A dowelled carcase

Between a dovetailed joint and mere nailing there is a halfway house, dowelling. This construction is useful where skill is limited or price is decisive. It is particularly useful for cabinets housing technical equipment, for example, where an elaborate job is not necessary.

A flush corner joint (Fig 237) is weak when dowelled, the holes being too close to the end (Fig 238). This means tops must overhang ends (Fig 239) or ends must be extended above the top (Fig 240). This latter can permit a back rail (Fig 241) which prevents items from slipping down behind.

A straightforward dowel joint (Fig 242) gives no resistance to warping. A shallow housing, stopped at the ends (Fig 243), is an altogether stronger joint and is the main joint of a dowelled carcase. To construct it, cramp together the sides or ends and mark the total length and the shelf positions with a sharp

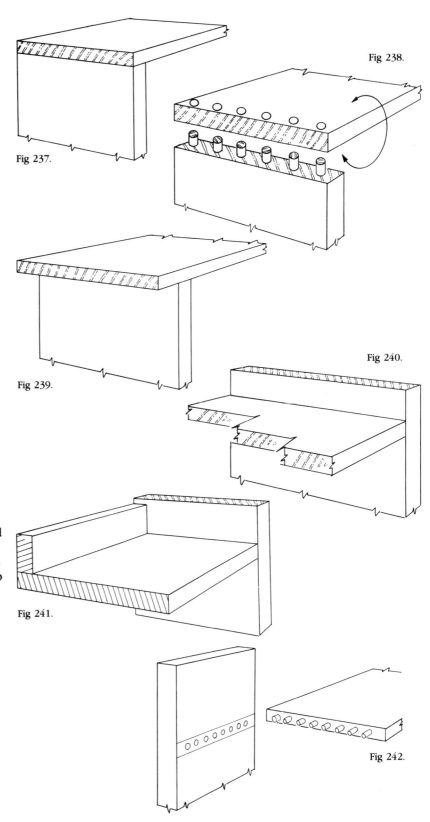

Fig 237.

Fig 238.

Fig 239.

Fig 240.

Fig 241.

Fig 242.

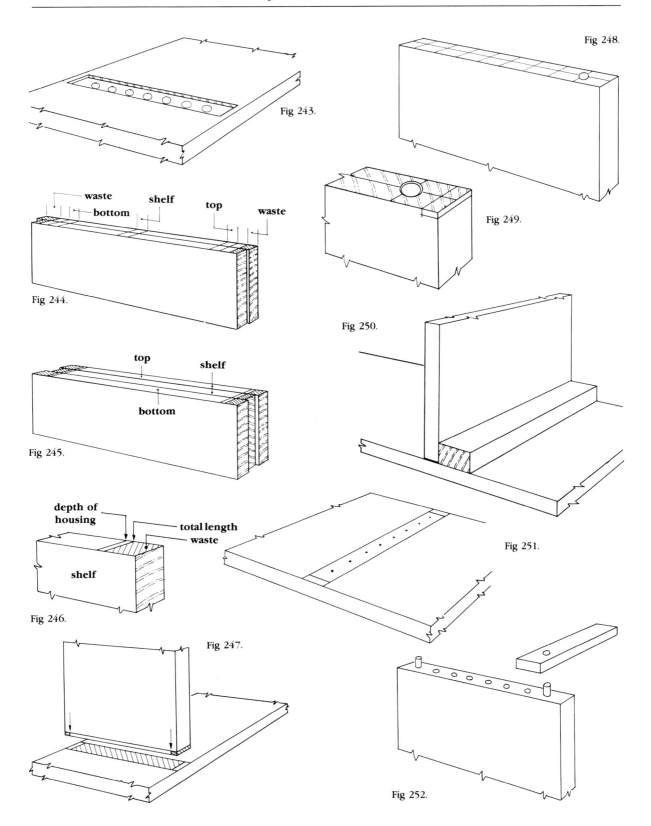

Fig 243.

Fig 248.

Fig 249.

waste
bottom
shelf
top
waste

Fig 244.

Fig 250.

top
shelf
bottom

Fig 245.

Fig 251.

depth of
housing
total length
waste
shelf

Fig 246.

Fig 247.

Fig 252.

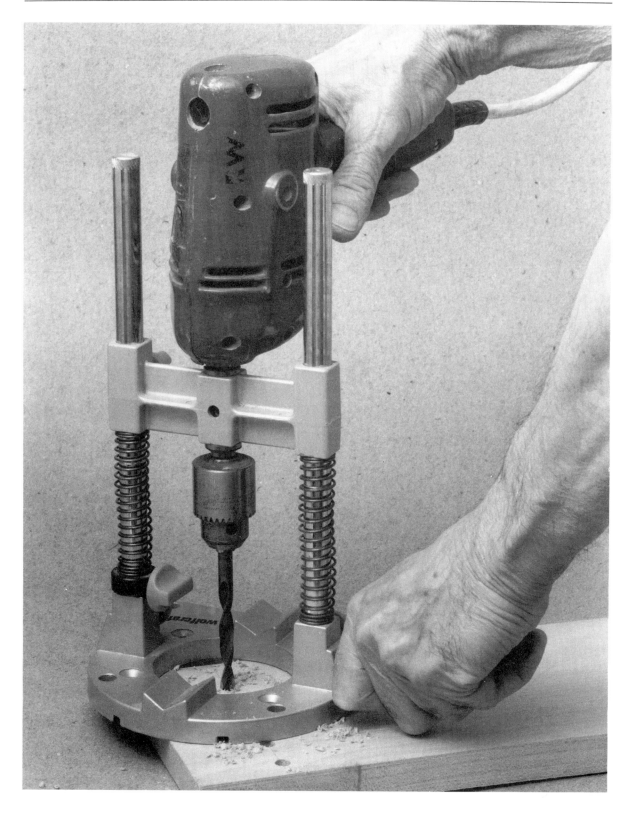

pencil (Fig 244). Separate and square onto the true face, which is always inside on a carcase. Cramp together the shelves and other horizontal members (Fig 245), mark the total length and the depth of the housing (Fig 246). Separate, square onto all four sides, saw off carefully and plane the ends if necessary. Gauge on *all* the pieces the stop which conceals the housing, 6mm ($\frac{1}{4}$in.) is generally right (Fig 247).

Mark the position of the dowels on the ends of all the relevant pieces. Many readers will use a dowelling jig of some sort so the maker's instructions will be followed here. Those working without the jig will mark the positions on a gauged centre line; there is no need for precise spacing (Fig 248). Drill the holes using an electric drill with a depth stop and countersink very slightly (Fig 249). Dowel marker pins are inserted or else the markings from Fig 248 must be transferred to the matching component.

Cramp a batten along the joint line (Fig 250) and hold or cramp the mating component to it, with the marker pins in place, and tap smartly to obtain the centre marks (Fig 251). Drill on these, preferably using a drilling machine. When the boards are too wide, a tool such as the Wolfcraft drill guide is handy (see photograph 36). On this drilling it is vital to use a depth stop.

Prepare the dowels as previously described on p.62, or use manufactured dowels.

36 Dowelling—an aid to ensure a drilling is vertical and to a constant depth

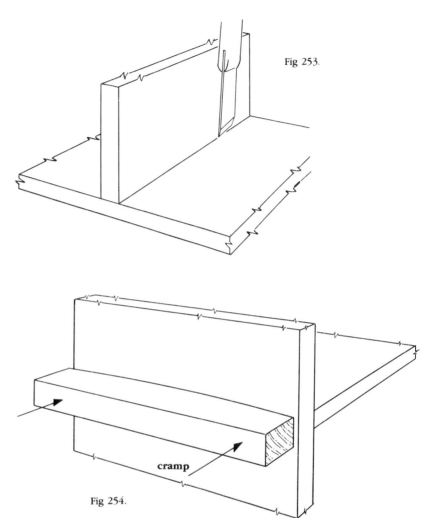

Fig 253.

cramp

Fig 254.

Glue two of these in each joint (Fig 252). Prepare a small height gauge as shown, fit it over each dowel and tap level. One overlong dowel can cause a great deal of bother when glueing up.

Knock each joint tightly together and mark the housing width accurately with a sharp knife (Fig 253). Be sure that the knife gets into the corner. The waste is removed from the housing either by power router or by chisel and hand router. The edges should be cut in the knife line with a wide chisel. Remove the notches on the mating parts to give the stopped housings. Saw close to the mark and finish with a sharp chisel wider than the wood thickness.

Cramp up the carcase dry, checking for a good fit. Dismantle, clean up and polish all inside surfaces. Make sure that the shelves do not become too thin in this process. Glue in the remaining dowels and remove the excess glue.

The cramping blocks used should be made for the job with

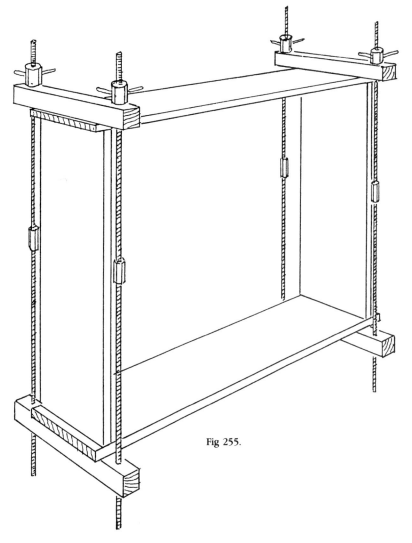

Fig 255.

some care. Do not use odd scraps which happen to be lying around. They must be slightly curved (Fig 254) to ensure pressure in the centre of the carcase sides, otherwise the sides may glue up bowed. If sufficient sash cramps are not available, drill the blocks and cramp by using screwed rods, nuts and washers. 12mm ($\frac{1}{2}$in.) is suggested, running in holes of 14mm (9/16in.) (Fig 255).

Provision for backs is considered on pp.97–102.

A dovetailed carcase

The dovetail is the traditional and strongest corner joint. Some of its various forms are shown in Fig 256 but of these only the common (or through) dovetail and the lap dovetail can be considered as basic skills. The great advantage of a dovetail construction is that there are no protruding corners. The essence of the common dovetail is its 'cornerliness', which means that it shows off well on the top

corner of a cabinet (Fig 257), but as a bottom corner (Fig 258) the row of rectangles is only dull and unattractive. For this reason the common dovetail is used for a top corner and the lap dovetail for the bottom. A lap dovetail at the top (Fig 259) has nothing to commend it and is easily confused with the inferior machine-made lap dovetail.

There are a number of variations of the common dovetail of which the simplest and one of the most effective is grouping or clustering the dovetails (Fig 260). Groups of two or three are most successful. On a wide job four is perhaps the limit which allows the pattern to be easily recognized. It is particularly important that the pattern should be clear at a first glance.

As well as the spacing, the proportions of dovetails are an important and to some extent a personal matter. As a guide the greatest width of the pins should be less than the thickness of the timber used (Fig 261). Big pins have an ugly appearance which larger tails do not have. In planning dovetails, think ahead to the final glue-up. A glue-up as Fig 262 presents no problems but Fig 263 calls for a more elaborate glue-up procedure, possibly a two-stage operation.

Where a groove, rebate, moulding or inlay is to be incorporated into a dovetail joint it is customary to mitre the corner (Fig 264). An alternative to this, generally reserved for back corners where it is often used for grooved or rebated backs, is to reduce the thickness of one tail and to extend the matching shoulder line (Fig 265).

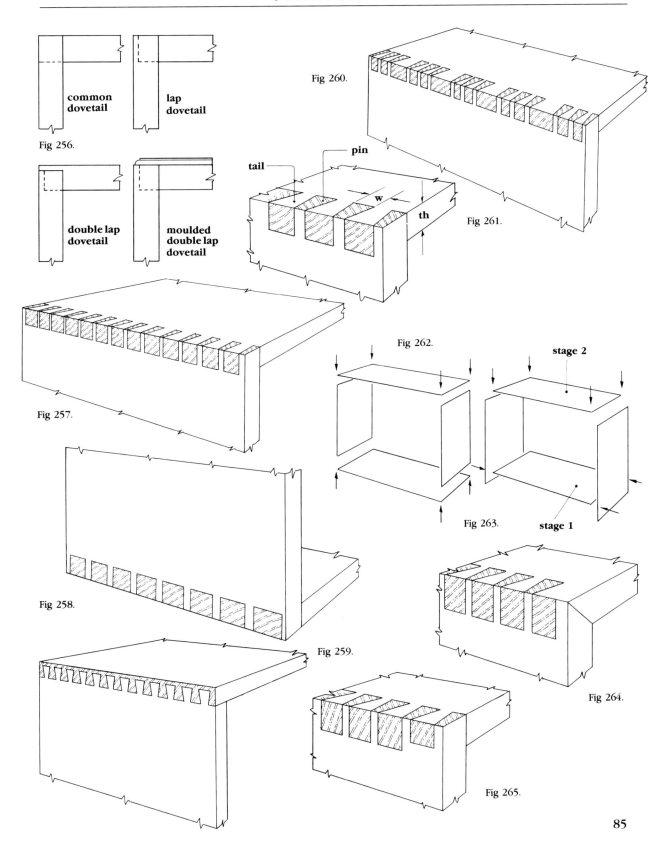

common dovetail

lap dovetail

Fig 256.

double lap dovetail

moulded double lap dovetail

Fig 260.

tail

pin

w

th

Fig 261.

Fig 257.

Fig 262.

stage 2

Fig 263.

stage 1

Fig 258.

Fig 259.

Fig 264.

Fig 265.

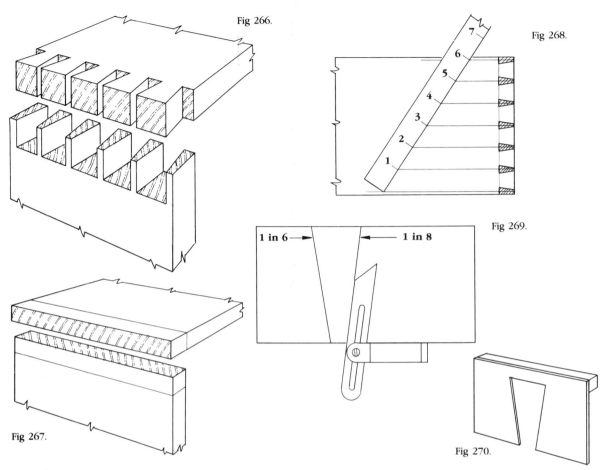

Fig 266.

Fig 268.

Fig 269.

Fig 267.

1 in 6

1 in 8

Fig 270.

Marking and cutting dovetails

The common or through dovetail

This is illustrated in Fig 266.
Material for dovetailing should
be produced very slightly over
the required thickness to allow
for later cleaning up. The ends
should be a thin 1mm (1/16in.)
overlength. Preferably one
should shoot the ends to give a
good surface on which to mark
and from which to gauge. (Some
workers prefer to saw only and
then to square rather than
gauge.)

Using the cutting gauge (see
photograph 37) mark a line at
each end of each piece a thin
1mm (1/16in.) greater than the
thickness of the matching piece

(Fig 267). The end pin must be
a little greater than half of the
other pins (Fig 268), so pencil a
mark down each edge about
3mm ($\frac{1}{8}$in.) in from the edge.
Increase this for a very wide
joint. Having decided on the
number of pins, divide up with
parallel lines as illustrated and
draw in the centre lines. Set a
sliding bevel to the dovetail
angle (Fig 269): a slope of 1 in 6
is customary for softwood and
1 in 8 for hardwoods. A small
piece of ply, suitably marked,
can be kept for this purpose.
Alternatively a dovetail marker
can be made (Fig 270) from
sheet metal, plastic laminate or
clear acrylic sheet. Additionally
the ends of the marker serve as

a small square.

Complete the marking out as
in Fig 268. Set out the pins
centrally on the pencil lines. If
possible their width should be
just greater than the chisel. On
woods with a 'soapy' feel to
them, which do not take pencil
well, wipe the sealer brush
across the face to give a bite for
the pencil. Square the lines onto
the end grain and shade in the
waste. This is important to
prevent the wrong part from
being sawn out or the saw
being on the wrong side of the
line. The marked tails should
now look as Fig 271.

Saw the tails up to but not
astride the line (Fig 272A). Do
not saw clear of the line with

86

37 The cutting gauge. In addition to its uses for cutting small rebates and veneer strips, this gauge is vital for marking across the grain where an ordinary marking gauge will tear

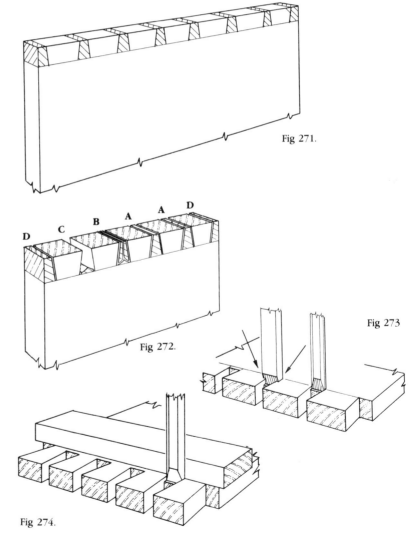

Fig 271.

Fig 272.

Fig 273

Fig 274.

the intention of paring down later; it is not as accurate as good sawing and is very time-wasting. A sharp saw is needed but it is not necessary always to use a dovetail saw. In view of the difficulty of sharpening very fine saws, keep the dovetail saw for fine dovetails and use a tenon saw for larger ones; the bulk of waste is removed by a coping saw. Saw down the centre towards the corners (Fig 272*B* and *C*), which avoids bruising the corner with the back of the blade as would be the case if the original sawcut was followed. Beware of cutting into the dovetail. The end pins (Fig 272*D*) are removed by sawing very close to the shoulder line then cutting back with a chisel wider than the wood thickness.

When cutting the pins back to the line a bevel-edged chisel must be used; a firmer chisel with square edges (Fig 273) will damage the dovetail. The last fine cut is made with the chisel in the gauge line. Chop halfway

from each side. Accuracy can be guaranteed by cramping a block along the gauge line (Fig 274). It is worth making a permanent aid for this purpose. Glue on a piece of fine glasspaper set in slightly from the edges (Fig 275).

To mark the pins hold the components together (Fig 276). Be sure before marking that the joints are numbered or lettered. Fig 277 shows a useful aid for cramping the components securely together while marking; a pair of these is required for a wide joint. Use a sharp awl for the marking, or improvise by using one made from an old steel knitting needle or a very large darning needle. A bent version is helpful to get into small sockets (Fig 278). Some workers chalk the end grain to obtain clearer markings. Square down these markings to the gauge lines on both sides and carefully mark the waste (Fig 279). Make the vertical sawcuts and remove the waste as with the tails. Assembly can be facilitated by slightly chamfering the entering corners (Fig 280).

39 Removing waste with the coping saw—working in this position the saw should cut in the push stroke

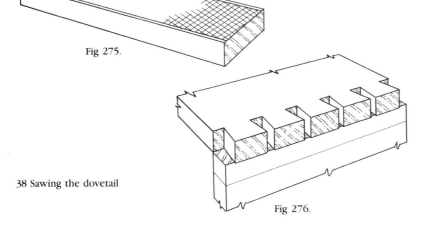

Fig 275.

38 Sawing the dovetail

Fig 276.

Fig 277.

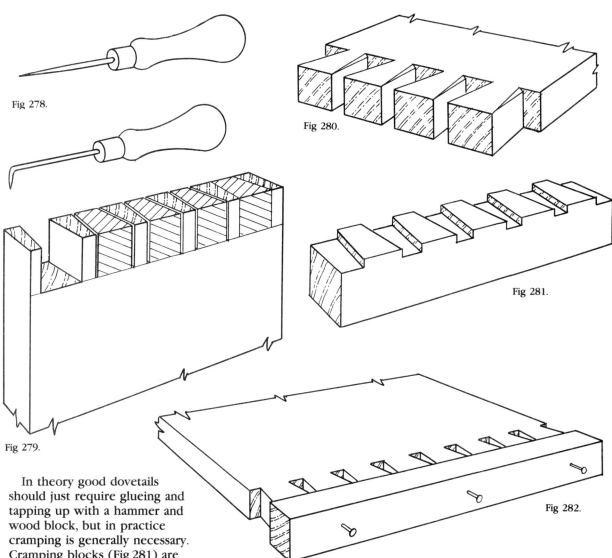

Fig 278.

Fig 280.

Fig 279.

Fig 281.

Fig 282.

In theory good dovetails should just require glueing and tapping up with a hammer and wood block, but in practice cramping is generally necessary. Cramping blocks (Fig 281) are prepared by scribing from the dovetails and cutting on the 'wrong' side of the lines, giving a series of pressure points just smaller than the dovetails. The blocks should be well waxed to prevent adhesion.

After glueing plane the joints level, always working inwards and taking off the inside corners of pins and tails with a chisel to prevent bursting out.

An alternative method of dovetailing is to prepare pins and tails a hair's breadth less than the wood thickness, glue, cramp up with plain blocks, then skim the carcase down to the joints. But the beginner is advised to use the first method described, though it requires a little more work.

Before assembly, if polishing, protect pins, tails and sockets from the polish by covering them with plastic tape. If to be unpolished, lay a strip of tape up to the shoulder line to prevent the glue from sticking. If dovetails are not to be assembled immediately they can be protected from damage, particularly at the vulnerable corners, by tacking on a lath, the nails entering between the dovetails (Fig 282).

40 Paring the shoulder to line. The chisel must be slightly wider than the wood thickness

90

Marking and cutting lap dovetails

The lap dovetail has three major applications: the bottom joint of carcases, the top joint of carcases which have applied tops, and the joint for drawer fronts.

The marking out and cutting is very similar in each case. At the bottom of the carcase it is customary to strengthen the joint by putting a small dovetail at each end (Fig 283). The remaining dovetails can be quite large and the pins also quite substantial.

Applied tops (i.e. unjointed to the carcase) may be inset or overhanging. They are screwed to a front and back rail and in rare cases to a centre rail also. Generally one large dovetail is used (Fig 284). Occasionally two tails are used. Often the width of the rail is increased at the joint by the addition of a triangular fillet, shown dotted. This enables several dovetails to be arranged.

Drawer dovetails (Fig 285) are dealt with later. The pins are generally much finer than in carcase joints. In Victorian times cabinet makers had an obsession with making excessively fine pins, which though an exercise in fine workmanship greatly reduced the strength of the joint.

When making lap dovetails plane both ends, preferably on the shooting board. Gauge the component containing the sockets with the cutting gauge (Fig 286A), which is minutely greater than the thickness of the tail component, A. Set the gauge to the lap distance, B, on both pieces. Cut the tails in the manner already described then offer them up to the matching component. The pairs should be numbered or lettered before any further marking is made (Fig 287). Cramp the pieces together and mark with a sharp awl. Shade the waste and begin sawing. Having sawn the pins, the bulk of the waste can be removed in a variety of ways, such as the power router with its fence, a forstner or sawtooth bit in the drilling machine, the coping saw cutting from corner to corner, or by weakening cut with the tenon saw (Fig 288).

Complete the sockets with the chisel. First cut across the grain (Fig 289A) then cleave off as at *a*. Continue in this way to the final cut, *B*, followed by *b*. Formerly the entire waste used

41 The machine dovetail—cut by expensive machinery or by attachments. This produces rather a monotonous finish

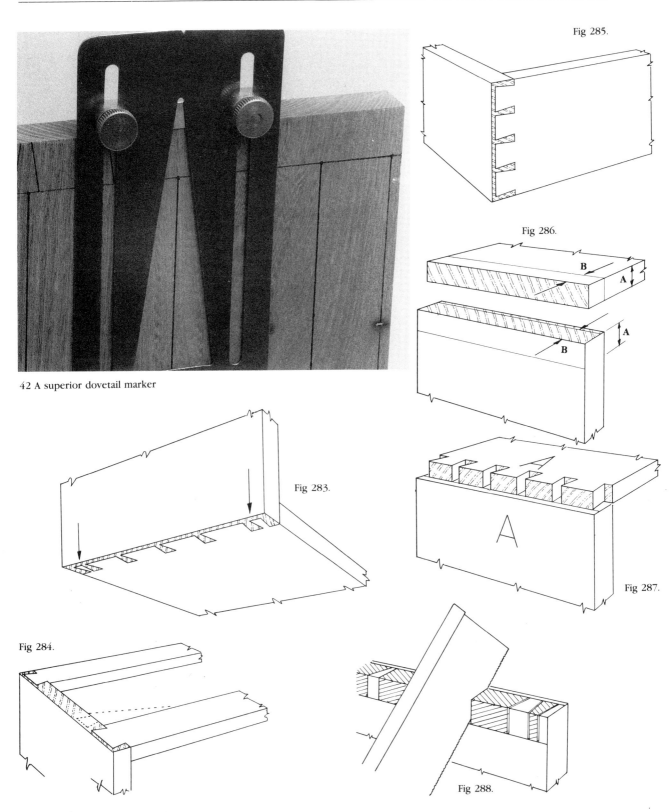

Fig 285.

Fig 286.

Fig 283.

Fig 287.

Fig 284.

Fig 288.

42 A superior dovetail marker

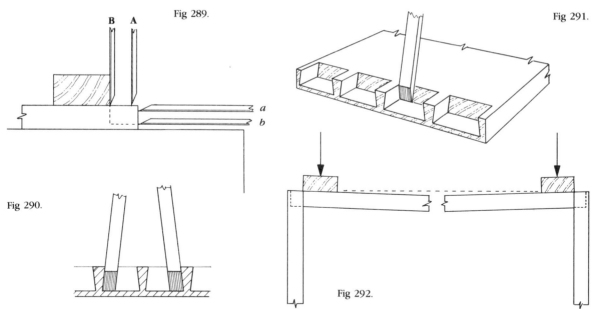

Fig 289.

Fig 291.

Fig 290.

Fig 292.

to be removed by chisel only with a little paring at the sides of the sockets. This method is still used for dovetails too small to permit mechanical waste removal. If the work is held some distance in from the bench edge, as shown, the bench top gives some guidance to the chisel, *a* and *b*, in keeping it horizontal. The final cut, *B*, is again made against a cramped block.

Cleaning out the corners presents a problem, particularly in the case of small dovetail sockets. For this it is useful to grind a pair of chisels to an angle slightly greater than the dovetail angle (Fig 290). These make a very clean job of the corners (Fig 291). The tails can be slightly chamfered to ease entry and the glue-up follows the same lines as for the common dovetail. In most cases cramping blocks will be necessary. The short cut of using a plain block set just clear of the dovetail (Fig 292) can cause the dovetailed component to set bowed.

Shelves

Shelves can be fixtures, often helping to strengthen the carcase, or they can be adjustable. The former will be considered first. The simple or stopped housing joint (Fig 293), has no strength, being all end grain glueing, however it does prevent the shelf from warping. The stronger dovetail housing or tapered dovetail housing is not a basic skill. The best method for the beginner is to tenon the shelves into the sides. Through tenons are particularly suited to the coarser grained woods, oak, ash, elm and chestnut, but not to the finer mahoganies and similar woods.

Fig 294 shows a bad example of tenoning. The very wide mortices cut across so many fibres that the component is severely weakened. Unfortunately examples of this are common. The joint at Fig 295 is both constructionally more sound and aesthetically more pleasing. Fig 296 shows the most effective form of this

joint, which combines a housing with the tenons. The front corner should be *stopped* to conceal the joint. At the rear the joint may or may not be stopped, according to preference and the construction chosen.

Fig 297 shows a common variation where the shelf is set back from the carcase front. This also permits a moulding on the shelf edge when the carcase itself is plain. It is essential where a door is fitted inside the carcase or when sliding glass doors are used. The gauging for this is very simply arranged. A block is produced (Fig 298) of a thickness the same as the set-in. This is slipped over the marking gauge. The shelf is gauged with the block and the carcase sides without it.

When tenons are brought through, giving a very strong carcase, they are generally wedged (Fig 299). Fig 300 shows how the wedges are mass produced from a small block, sawn to the tenon thickness. Make the cuts with a fine saw then saw off the entire strip. Making them individually by paring with a chisel is time-wasting and can be dangerous. Note that sawcuts are made for the wedges, which are not driven in at the ends of the mortice in the manner of the joiner. The mortice is opened out slightly to accept the wedges.

There are many methods of supporting adjustable and removable shelves including quite a number of commercial systems. One of the simplest is Fig 301. However this does not prevent the shelf from sliding when in use. This defect is remedied by glueing a small strip to the rear edge of the shelf to fit into a gap behind the bearer (Fig 302). In a backless carcase a similar strip is needed at the front (Fig 303). This has the further advantage that thinner material may be used for the shelf while retaining the appearance of thickness. Moulding may be required on this thickened edge.

For better quality work a more sophisticated method is recommended. Fig 304 shows notches cut into the under face of the shelf, to accept turned supporting studs (Fig 305). These are usually 13mm ($\frac{1}{2}$in.) diameter with a 6mm ($\frac{1}{4}$in.) peg. Rosewood or a similar exotic wood is generally chosen.

It is worth making a metal drilling strip for adjustable shelves (Fig 306). It will always come in useful again. Carefully

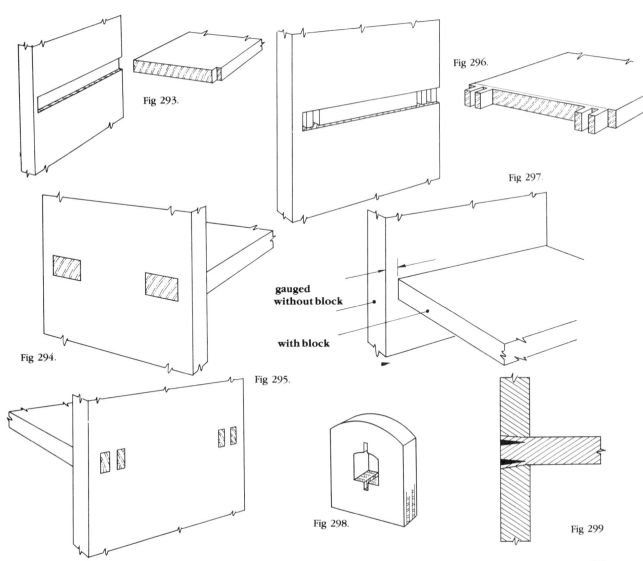

Fig 293.

Fig 296.

Fig 297.

Fig 294.

gauged
without block

with block

Fig 295.

Fig 298.

Fig 299

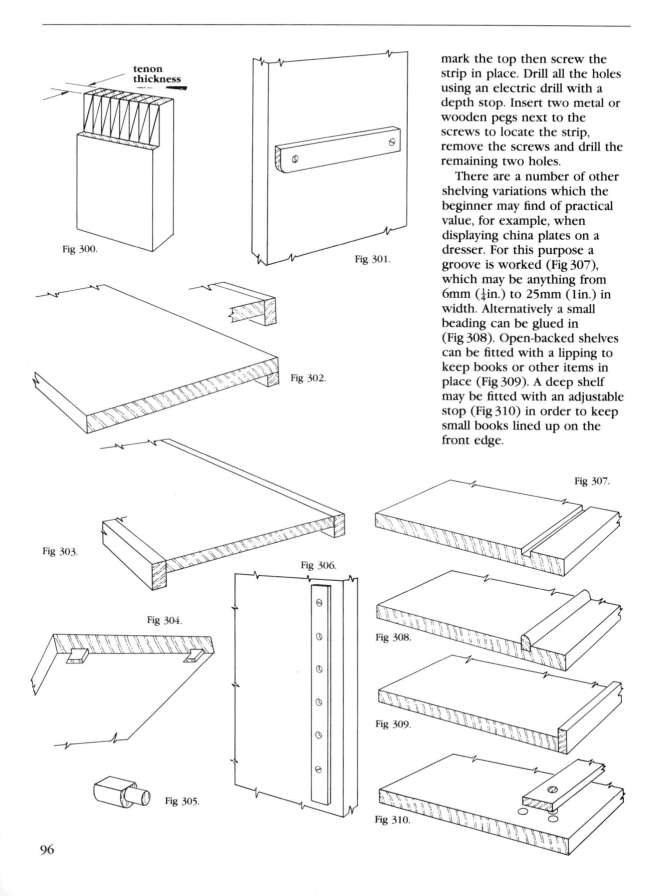

tenon
thickness

Fig 300.

Fig 301.

Fig 302.

Fig 303.

Fig 304.

Fig 305.

Fig 306.

Fig 307.

Fig 308.

Fig 309.

Fig 310.

mark the top then screw the strip in place. Drill all the holes using an electric drill with a depth stop. Insert two metal or wooden pegs next to the screws to locate the strip, remove the screws and drill the remaining two holes.

There are a number of other shelving variations which the beginner may find of practical value, for example, when displaying china plates on a dresser. For this purpose a groove is worked (Fig 307), which may be anything from 6mm ($\frac{1}{4}$in.) to 25mm (1in.) in width. Alternatively a small beading can be glued in (Fig 308). Open-backed shelves can be fitted with a lipping to keep books or other items in place (Fig 309). A deep shelf may be fitted with an adjustable stop (Fig 310) in order to keep small books lined up on the front edge.

Cabinet backs

A Victorian book on cabinet making states that the back of a cabinet or carcase should be framed and panelled: 'in inferior work a tongue and groove back may be fitted'. Since those days tongue and groove backs have become respectable, being preferred to backs of veneered plywood, plain plywood, chipboard, hardboard or no backs at all. The variety of backs and their methods of fitting are therefore considerable and worth exploring. It is assumed that the carcase itself is made from solid wood and that all the work can be done with hand tools or simple machine tools. In none of the examples given here are the backs glued to the carcase or the panels glued to the frame.

Fig 311 shows a fairly typical bookcase with the shelves removed. The back consists of a frame with a centre muntin and four horizontal rails. Six panels are grooved into the frame. Such a framed back is a most effective way to stiffen up a carcase. Fig 312 shows a section of a grooved frame taking flush panels, the most refined and advanced method, giving a smooth surface to the inside of the cabinet. In making a flush and beaded panel it is wise to minutely increase the panel thickness so that after the glue-up it can be cleaned exactly level with the frame. The bead should be scratched or cut very slightly below the finished surface to avoid the risk of planing a flat on it when cleaning up the surface.

The panel at Fig 313 is of solid wood fielded or thinned at the edges with a jack plane to fit the groove. The fielding

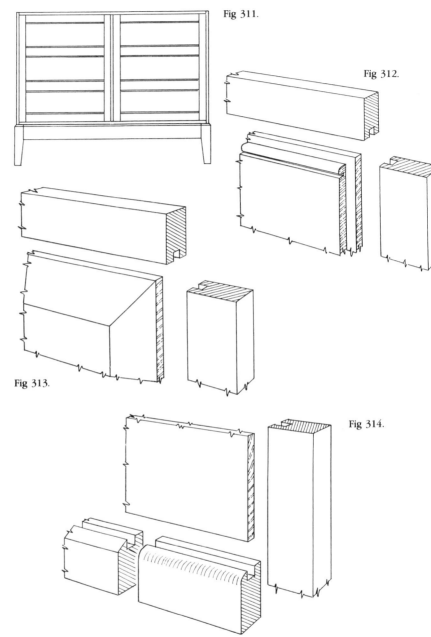

Fig 311.

Fig 312.

Fig 313.

Fig 314.

would be on the back or outside. A simpler form (Fig 314) is a plain solid wood or veneered ply panel. In each of these forms the grain would run horizontally. When the plain or fielded panel is used, it is advisable to shape the horizontal rails in Fig 314 either with a bevel or a quarter round. This looks less aggressive, collects dust less and is easier to clean.

The frame can be fitted to the carcase in several ways. In the simplest (Fig 315) the plain frame is fitted into a rebate in the carcase and is held by

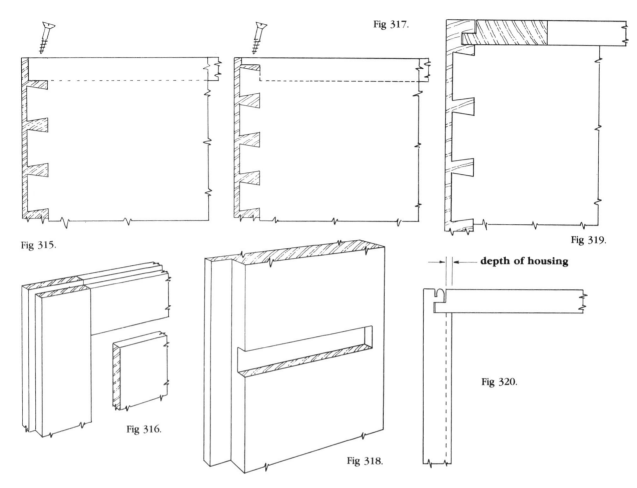

Fig 317.

Fig 315.

Fig 319.

depth of housing

Fig 320.

Fig 316.

Fig 318.

countersunk screws (brass for good-quality work) slightly angled. But the effect of this method is to move the first dovetail rather far in from the edge, thus weakening the joint. A better method (Figs 316 and 317) is to rebate the frame also, which enables the end dovetail to be placed nearer to the edge, making a stronger joint. Fig 318 shows how the rebate permits the housing for a shelf to come right through at the back, making cutting it easier when working with a hand or power router.

In Fig 319 the back is grooved in. The rebate is worked on the outside of the frame, forming the tongue to fit into the carcase groove. This is a neat arrangement but complicates the cutting of the shelf housings. By a combination of groove and rebate (Fig 320) the cutting of the housings is simplified. A small bead is sometimes worked on the carcase, if so it must be below the line of the shelf housing.

The bottom shelf or carcase bottom is usually set back to the line of the rebate or groove and the back screwed directly to this (Fig 321), which makes the glue-up simpler. The carcase only is glued, the back being applied later.

Provision must be made for the groove or housing in the corner joints of the carcase. Fig 322 shows a mitred rear corner, commonly used with through dovetails or comb (finger) joints. Alternatively, a dovetail (or sometimes a pin) can be shortened to take and conceal a groove (Fig 323); a lap dovetail, as in a drawer, is handled similarly. A double lap dovetail is a slightly simpler situation for grooving as the groove can run through in both components, being completely hidden when the joint is assembled (Fig 324). A rebate with this joint can only be arranged by mitring the corner. According to the relative thicknesses of the side

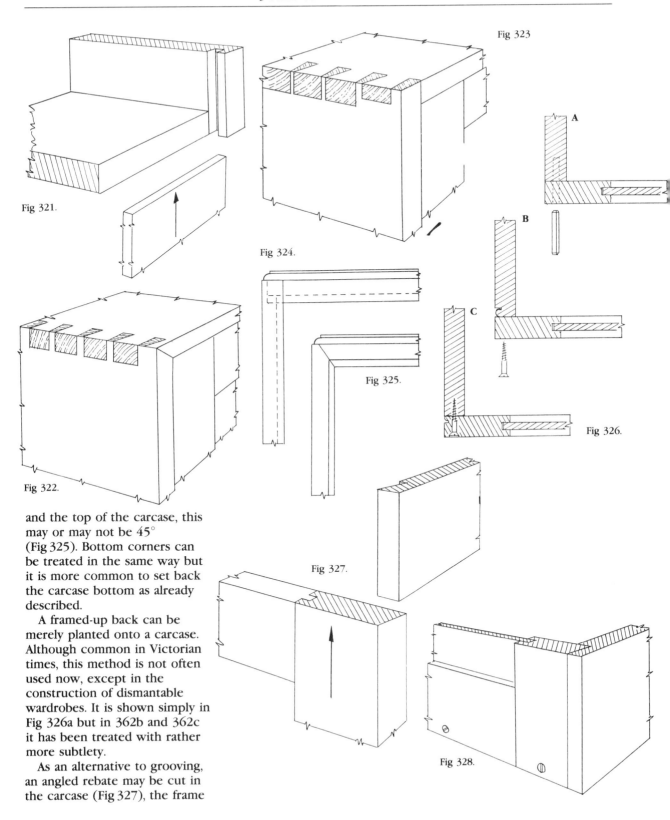

Fig 323

Fig 321.

Fig 324.

A

B

Fig 325.

C

Fig 326.

Fig 322.

Fig 327.

Fig 328.

and the top of the carcase, this may or may not be 45° (Fig 325). Bottom corners can be treated in the same way but it is more common to set back the carcase bottom as already described.

A framed-up back can be merely planted onto a carcase. Although common in Victorian times, this method is not often used now, except in the construction of dismantable wardrobes. It is shown simply in Fig 326a but in 362b and 362c it has been treated with rather more subtlety.

As an alternative to grooving, an angled rebate may be cut in the carcase (Fig 327), the frame being angled to match in the manner of a dovetail housing. A power router with a dovetail cutter will produce a very accurate rebate. Using a very finely set smoothing plane, the frame can be eased in to a very fine fit (Fig 328). This is not commonly used but is very effective.

The tongue and groove back (Fig 329) can be made from the same material as the carcase or of a contrasting wood. Cedar is particularly attractive for carcase backs and gives out a pleasant odour. Fig 330 shows the bottom fixing, similar to that of the framed back. The tongue and groove back needs very careful planning, preferably full size for quality work. The two

end boards are different from the centre boards and from each other. Fig 331 clarifies this and gives the calculations for obtaining the component sizes. Allowance must be made for possible slight expansion. Shrinkage is quite easily obscured by the chosen style of decoration. Fig 332 gives some alternative forms.

None of these solutions is ideal in cases where the top and sometimes also the bottom of a carcase overlaps the side. This situation is common in dowelled constructions. Although a stopped groove can be made in the top with an electric router, traditional methods using the plough plane or even a small circular saw make this rather

messy. It is always preferable to run a groove right through. A neat alternative is to fit a narrow grooved rail top and bottom (Fig 333). In wall-mounted cabinets this makes a very convenient hanging rail. This style accepts all the types of panels so far described. Figs 334 and 335 indicate how a similar rail can be fitted to each shelf, making it possible either to fit individual panels or to construct a tongue and groove back from very short components.

Real show panels occur on items which will be seen from all sides, for example, the pedestal desk. Framed backs are nearly always the rule here. Panels are generally step-fielded

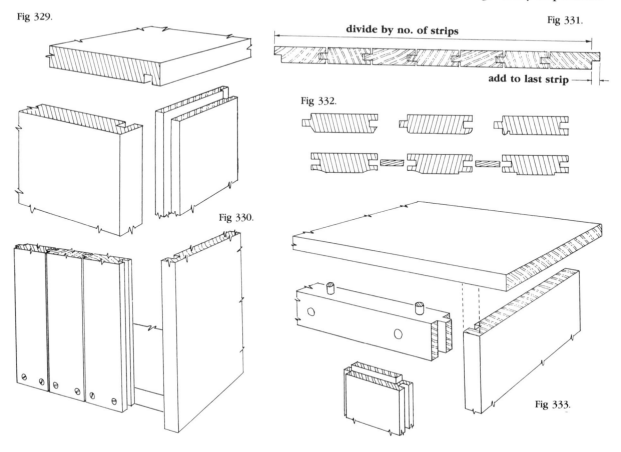

Fig 329.

Fig 331.

divide by no. of strips

add to last strip

Fig 332.

Fig 330.

Fig 333.

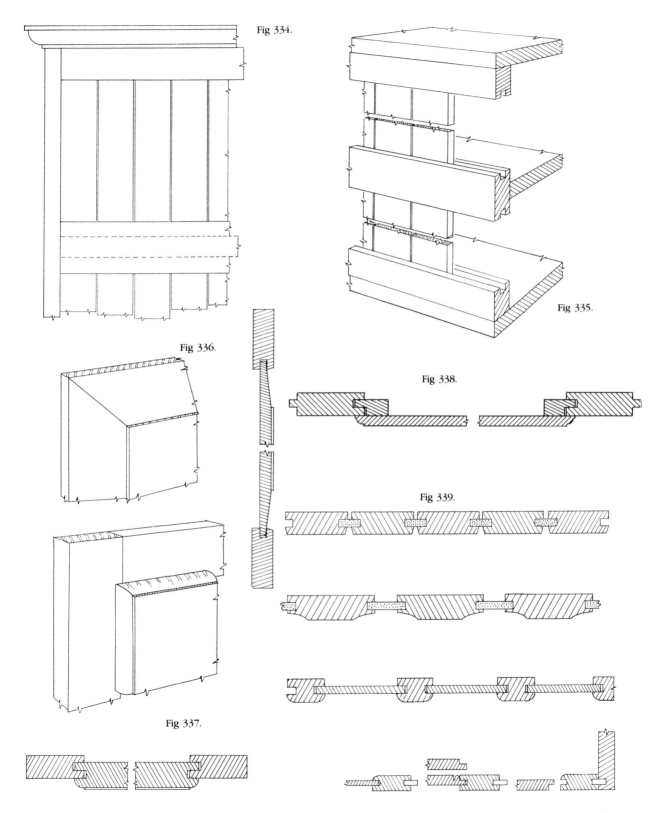

Fig 334.

Fig 335.

Fig 336.

Fig 338.

Fig 339.

Fig 337.

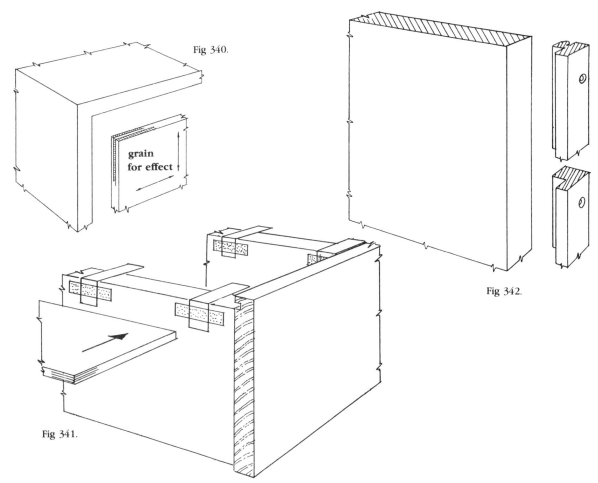

Fig 340.

grain
for effect

Fig 342.

Fig 341.

(Fig 336) though both flush and beaded panels are just as suitable. Raised panels (Fig 337) are another possibility; they are thick, heavy and expensive in wood, but can be more cheaply built up from thinner material (Fig 338). Flush tongue and groove panels, not necessarily in the conventional forms (Fig 339), are another.

Plywood panels are of course a much simpler job (Fig 340), although a good quality of ply and veneer are needed for the best class of work. A minimum thickness of 6mm ($\frac{1}{4}$in.) is suggested for all but the smallest carcases. The fitting is easier, the ply back being

merely grooved or rebated in. As ply is more flexible than a frame or tongue and groove boards, it is wise to screw also into the shelves or centre partition. Plywood does not countersink nicely, so countersunk or raised-head screws are recommended in conjunction with brass screwcup washers.

When a polished ply back, or for that matter a flush panelled back, is slid up into place in the grooves, there is a chance that the back of the shelf will scratch the panel. This can be avoided by setting the shelves back very slightly from the groove, although if the plywood

is bowed it may still be scratched. A better method is to fix small tabs of card to the back edge of the shelf with plastic tape (Fig 341). These act as spacers and can be removed when the back is in place.

Fig 342 shows how a groove can be produced by screwing a loose fillet to the carcase. The idea is to enable a grooved-in panel to be fitted after the carcase has been glued together. It can be quite plain and skimmed level after fixing or a small bead can be worked to mask the join. The method is useful when it is required to fit a back to a previously backless piece.

102

The carcase glue-up

Unless a large number of cramps is available and several helpers are to hand the glue-up should be kept as simple as possible. Several small operations involving, say, four sash cramps are easier and less trouble than one massive glue-up with a vast weight of ironmongery. All insides should be cleaned up, finishing with a scraper then successively finer grades of glasspaper. The polishing process should be completed, during which dovetails, tenons, mortices and housings should be protected with cellulose tape or masking tape.

A complete dry cramp-up should be made, checking that all tools, cramping blocks (slightly curved) and equipment likely to be needed are to hand, including winding strips and a diagonal lath. More wedges should be made than will actually be required and they should be kept in a secure container with a hammer nearby. Speed is of the essence in a large carcase glue-up. One adhesive manufacturer gives an assembly time of 10 minutes; movement of the joints after that will affect adhesion. The

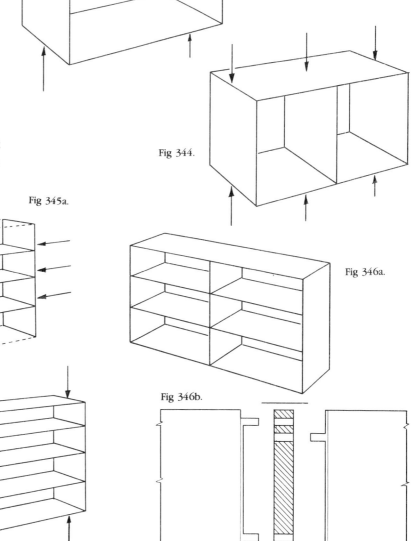

Fig 343.

Fig 344.

Fig 345a.

Fig 345b.

Fig 346a.

Fig 346b.

103

adherents of scotch glue need a warm, draught-free workshop and facility to warm the glueing areas; some workers now do this with an electric paint stripper. Two sawing stools or folding trestles support the carcase nicely, giving space for the cramp bars and access all round.

Before dismantling for the glue-up, rub wax polish into all the corners. This prevents exuding glue from sticking. If the interior has been varnished, the wax can easily be removed with white spirit, since washing off glue with hot water is inclined to leave permanent traces. It is obviously better to have arranged for a grooved-in or rebated back rather than a glued-in one as this simplifies the glue-up.

A simple box carcase (Fig 343) presents no problems. Supported on stools or boxes, top and bottom can be glued in together by vertical cramping. One or two vertical partitions (Fig 344) can be dealt with in the same way.

The introduction of fixed shelves complicates matters. In the first stage the shelves are glued to the sides with horizontal cramping. The top and bottom are knocked on dry (Fig 345a). In the second stage (Fig 345b) the top and bottom are glued on with vertical cramping.

Fig 346a illustrates both these features together. The joints into the vertical partition need careful planning. The tenons of each pair of shelves need to be staggered (Fig 346b). In the first stage, glue shelves, sides and partition with dry top and bottom (Fig 347a). At the second stage, add top and bottom (Fig 347b). The glue-up

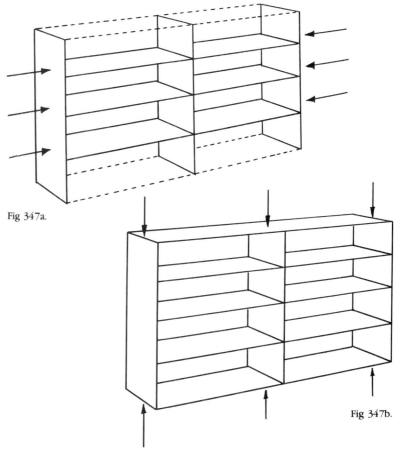

Fig 347a.

Fig 347b.

is easier when the shelves are staggered. Partition and one side are the first stage of glueing (Fig 348), followed by the second end (Fig 349) both with dry top and bottom. Top and bottom follow as the third stage, as in Fig 347b. By planning adjustable shelves the glue-up is much simpler. In large carcases such as tall bookcases, making one or more shelves as fixtures gives rigidity to the carcase, while the rest are adjustable.

When wedges are used, notched cramping blocks are necessary (Fig 350). The carcase is glued up without the wedges, checked for square and for wind, then one by one the cramping blocks are slid sideways, just sufficiently for the

wedges to be driven in, then returned.

In addition to examining the fit of the joints, test the carcase for twist and squareness. Use large winding strips to test for twist, and take care that they do not pick up glue. A try-square does not give sufficient accuracy so test squareness by means of a pointed diagonal lath and pencil (Fig 351). If two marks are made, the true diagonal is midway between them so adjust the cramping blocks slightly to achieve this. A cramping arrangement (see Fig 255) of heavy wood blocks, 12mm ($\frac{1}{2}$in.) screwed rods with nuts and washers, is a useful substitute for sash cramps or can supplement them. It is

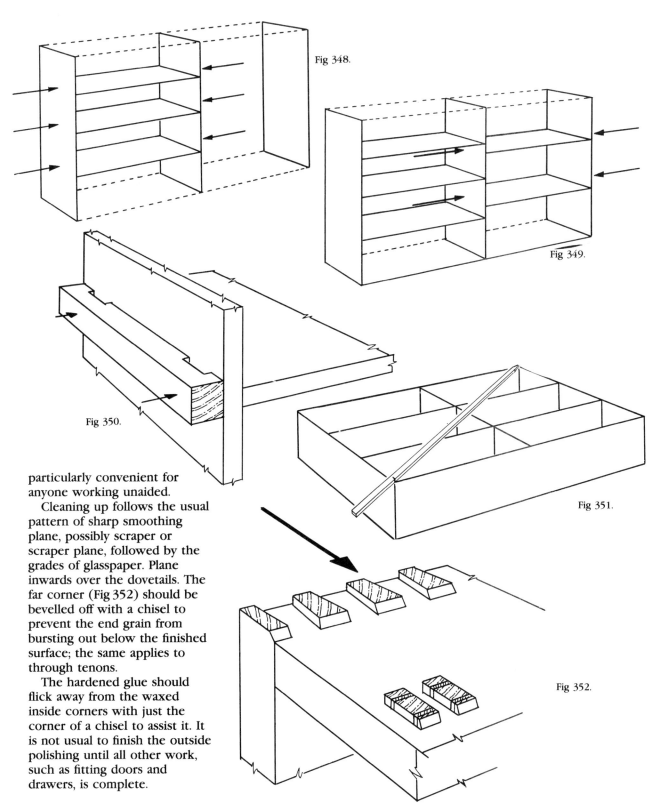

Fig 348.

Fig 349.

Fig 350.

Fig 351.

particularly convenient for anyone working unaided.

Cleaning up follows the usual pattern of sharp smoothing plane, possibly scraper or scraper plane, followed by the grades of glasspaper. Plane inwards over the dovetails. The far corner (Fig 352) should be bevelled off with a chisel to prevent the end grain from bursting out below the finished surface; the same applies to through tenons.

The hardened glue should flick away from the waxed inside corners with just the corner of a chisel to assist it. It is not usual to finish the outside polishing until all other work, such as fitting doors and drawers, is complete.

Fig 352.

Door types

In making plain or flush doors the obvious choice of material appears to be a well-chosen board of solid wood (Fig 353). However this is no solution since the wood may swell or shrink, spoiling the fit, or warp, making any fit impossible. A stable, light door suitable for painting or lower-quality work can be made from a mitred frame to which are glued two sheets of thin ply (Fig 354).

A heavier and more robust door is shown in Fig 355. Here a stronger frame is dowelled or tenoned together with two ply skins. Extra cross members are added to stiffen the door. Air holes are drilled in the cross members and in the bottom rail to equalize air pressure inside and outside. Such cross members must not be too far apart, nor should the ply be too thin (minimum 6mm (¼in.)), otherwise an impression of the framing may show through.

A door from multi-ply or blockboard is extremely stable, but the edges are unattractive and do not take the hinge screws well. Such a door is generally lipped (Fig 356). The lipping may be butted or mitred at the corners. The tongue is essential for good adhesion, particularly on the end grain of blockboard. The lipping may be applied to veneered material but for better work the lipping is concealed by veneering the whole face after the lippings have been glued and planed flush. Lippings must be made from thoroughly dry material, otherwise shrinkage will take place and the lipping will show through the veneer.

Good-quality handwork makes frequent use of the framed and panelled door (Fig 357), the inner edge of which is moulded or chamfered. The following illustrations show some of the possible combinations of panel and frame.

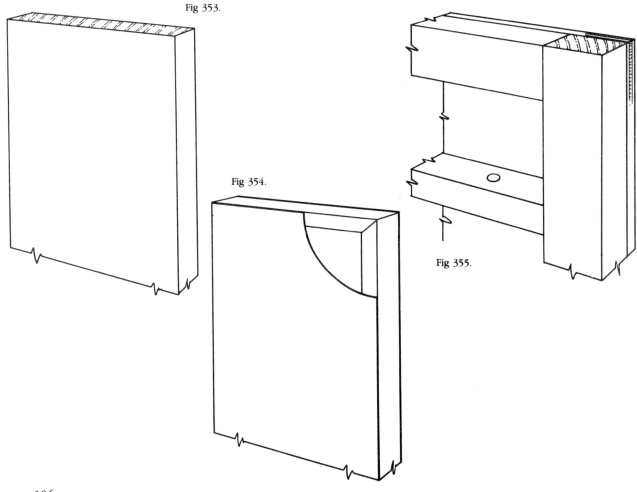

Fig 353.

Fig 354.

Fig 355.

106

Fig 356.

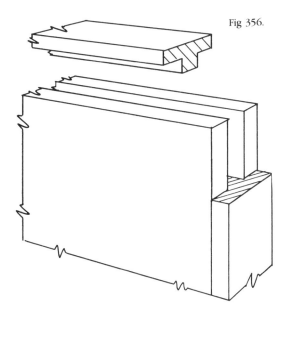

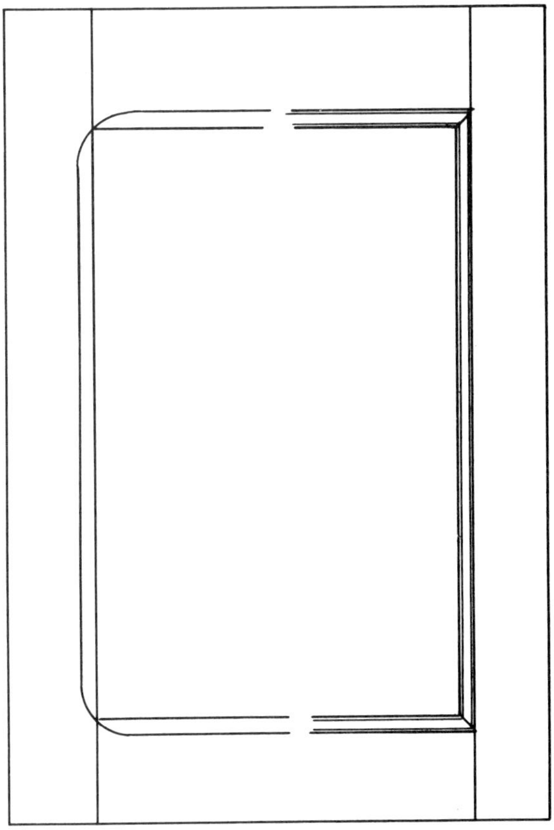

Fig 357.

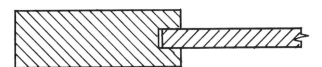

Fig 358. The simplest form. A solid wood or veneered plywood panel in a grooved frame.

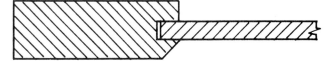

Fig 360. The outside corner chamfered.

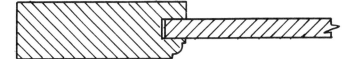

Fig 359. The outside corner moulded.

Fig 361. The panel fitted into a rebate and held there with a beading. This method is commercially popular as the panel can be polished before assembly. This is also the method for fixing glass panels.

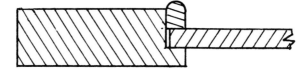

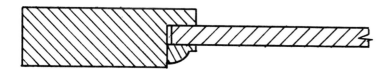

Fig 362. This less common form has a more decorative moulding fitted on the outside of the door.

Fig 363. A plain frame to which is added a raised 'bolection' moulding on the outside and a bead on the inside.

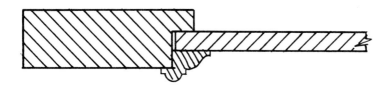

Fig 364. The bolection moulding combined with a rebate. Bolection moulding is generally bought in. It is not as common as it used to be, but specialists in hardwood mouldings generally produce several varieties, normally for the reproduction market.

Fig 365. A simple fielding, using a jack plane, is not very common, although it is still a favourite with some designer-craftsmen on grounds of speed and economy. It is frequently used on the inside of a door to thin down a panel which appears plain on the outside.

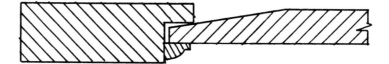

Fig 366. The step fielding, sometimes with two steps, also remains popular with hand craftsmen. A strip of wood is cramped to the panel, acting as a fence and the waste is removed—on a small panel with a large shoulder plane and on larger panels with a rebate plane. The ideal tool is the Record iron rebate plane No 010 or the Stanley equivalent. The thickness is gauged on the edges and the step is clearly marked with a cutting gauge. An alternative method of working (Figs 367 and 368) is to cut a narrow groove by plough, router or circular saw and then plane off the waste.

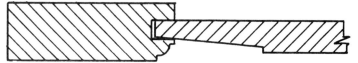

Fig 366.

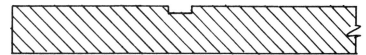

Fig 367.

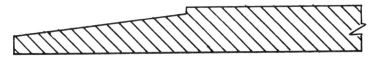

Fig 368.

Fig 369. The flush panel illustrated has already been described under 'Cabinet Backs'.

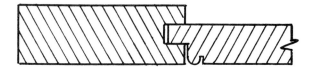

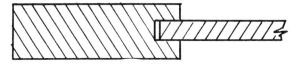

Fig 370. The flush tongue and groove panel is a variation of this.

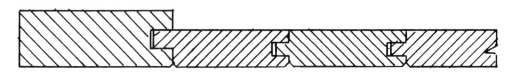

Fig 371. The raised panel with a moulding or bevel requires thicker material, so although it looks attractive, it may be rejected on grounds of weight or expense. At the dry cramp-up the frame must be well-fitting and flush since it is very inconvenient to work on it after the glue-up with the panel in place. The frame should be cramped up dry, checked for squareness and skimmed over the joints. Then, working from this face, cut the grooves.

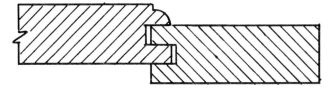

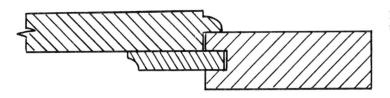

Fig 372. The panel can be considerably thinned if an applied tongue is glued on.

Fig 373. The panel can be thinned further if the applied components contain both tongue and groove.

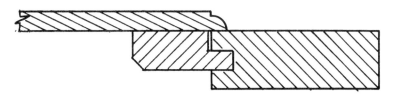

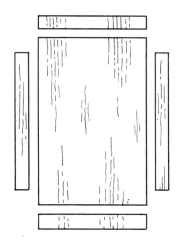

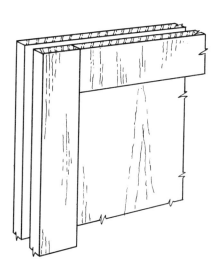

Fig 374. The grain of the applied strips must run in the same direction as that of the panel and ideally should be cut from the same board for a good grain match. The harsh inside corner can be removed by working a suitable moulding before glueing on.

Fig 375. A pair of doors requires a little thought at the planning stage; while the stiles (uprights) will appear to be of the same width, the closing arrangement necessitates that one inner stile is wider than the other three.

Fig 376. Where a beading is worked on the outer door both of the closing stiles will be wider than the hinge stiles. This method has the advantage that a small inaccuracy in fitting can be concealed since it does not demand such meticulous work at the closing edges.

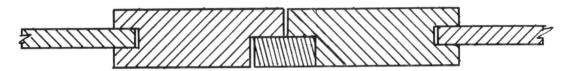

Fig 377. When a number of doors is planned, work can be saved by making all the stiles the same width, routing a rebate in each closing edge then glueing in a prepared strip to half of them.

Fig 378. This is a convenient solution for smaller doors, particularly on built-in or painted work. Multi-ply can be used or two pieces of thinner veneered ply can be glued together. Thicker, solid wood hingeing and closing strips are grooved, moulded and glued on, giving adequate material for hinges, catches, etc. The top and bottom edges of the panel are left without additions.

111

The framed door

(a) Grooved construction

The previous section showed some of the possibilities for the framed and panelled door. The constructional methods are all very similar, dividing very conveniently into rebated panels and grooved-in panels.

The simplest form (Fig 379) is a panel fitted to a plain grooved framework. Prepare the stiles and rails to width and thickness, mark the length from the carcase on one stile (Fig 380) and the shoulder length on one rail (Fig 381). Make a very slight allowance for cleaning up and fitting. Cramp the stiles together for marking out (Fig 382) then

separate. Set a mortice gauge to the chosen chisel and gauge the mortices (Fig 383). The mortice must be the same width as the groove or wider. There is no need to gauge the groove, though two pencil marks may serve as a reminder. The mortices can now be chopped and the haunch sockets worked (Fig 384).

Similarly, cramp the rails together and square them across at the shoulder length and tenon length (Fig 385). Separate the rails, square the lines round and saw off the waste (Fig 386). Gauge the tenons, using the same gauge setting, and shade the waste (Fig 387). Saw the cheeks of the

tenons (Fig 388), but do nothing further to the tenons at this stage.

Now work the grooves, using a plough or grooving plane, router or circular saw, producing stiles as in Fig 379 and rails as in Fig 389. Offer up a rail to a stile (Fig 390) and mark the haunch position. Set a gauge to this and mark all the tenons similarly. Use a small block the size of the groove depth to mark the length of the haunch (Fig 391). Saw out the haunch to produce the final tenon (Fig 379).

This construction produces a rather austere door which it is difficult to embellish. However

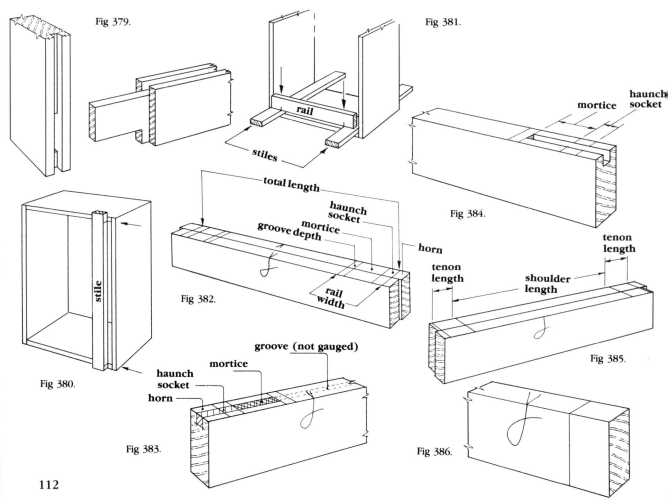

Fig 379.

Fig 381.

Fig 384.

Fig 382.

Fig 385.

Fig 380.

Fig 383.

Fig 386.

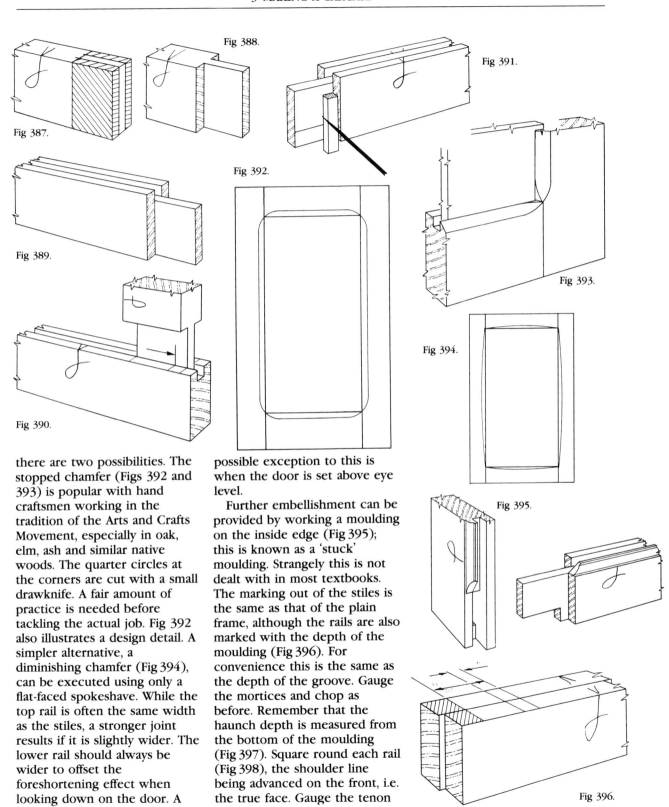

Fig 387.

Fig 388.

Fig 389.

Fig 390.

Fig 391.

Fig 392.

Fig 393.

Fig 394.

Fig 395.

Fig 396.

there are two possibilities. The stopped chamfer (Figs 392 and 393) is popular with hand craftsmen working in the tradition of the Arts and Crafts Movement, especially in oak, elm, ash and similar native woods. The quarter circles at the corners are cut with a small drawknife. A fair amount of practice is needed before tackling the actual job. Fig 392 also illustrates a design detail. A simpler alternative, a diminishing chamfer (Fig 394), can be executed using only a flat-faced spokeshave. While the top rail is often the same width as the stiles, a stronger joint results if it is slightly wider. The lower rail should always be wider to offset the foreshortening effect when looking down on the door. A possible exception to this is when the door is set above eye level.

Further embellishment can be provided by working a moulding on the inside edge (Fig 395); this is known as a 'stuck' moulding. Strangely this is not dealt with in most textbooks. The marking out of the stiles is the same as that of the plain frame, although the rails are also marked with the depth of the moulding (Fig 396). For convenience this is the same as the depth of the groove. Gauge the mortices and chop as before. Remember that the haunch depth is measured from the bottom of the moulding (Fig 397). Square round each rail (Fig 398), the shoulder line being advanced on the front, i.e. the true face. Gauge the tenon

Fig 397.

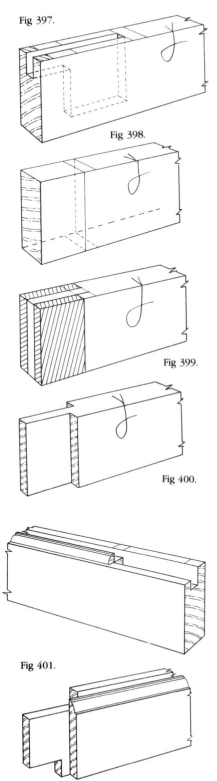

Fig 398.

Fig 399.

Fig 400.

Fig 401.

Fig 402.

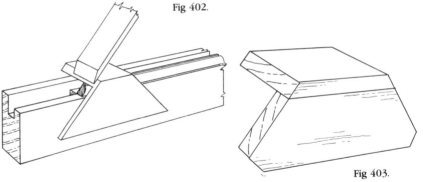

Fig 403.

and mark the waste (Fig 399). Saw only the cheeks (Fig 400). At this stage all the grooves are cut and the mouldings worked by router or scratch tool. Mark the haunch as with the plain frame, using a slightly wider small scribing block. Fig 401 shows the moulding on the stiles having been pared back to just short of the mortice end. All the moulding ends are mitred by careful paring with a sharp chisel and a mitre template (Fig 402). This can be bought or made from hardwood (Fig 403).

(b) Rebated construction

This construction (Fig 404) is similar to the previous one but some care is required in the marking out since the longer shoulder is now at the back.

Produce stiles and rails to their finished width and thickness then gauge the rebate sizes on the true edge and on the back, i.e. not the true face (Fig 405). Mark the stile length with allowance (Fig 380), cramp all the stiles together and mark out the joint (Fig 406). Mark the shoulder length of a rail with allowance, then cramp together the rails and mark the tenons (Fig 407).

Separate all the components, and saw off the waste from the

tenons (Fig 408), then gauge both the mortices (Fig 409) and the tenons (Fig 410). To avoid complications, one of the gauge lines should line up with the rebate gauging. Chop the mortices and work the haunch sockets (Fig 411). Saw the tenon cheeks and shoulders (Fig 412) but do nothing else at this stage.

The rebates can now be formed by hand using a rebate or shoulder plane, or mechanically by router, planer or circular saw. This completes the stiles (Fig 413) and brings the tenons to the stage shown in Fig 414. Mark the set-in for the haunch (Fig 415) and scribe its length from a template (Fig 416). In the event of a poor fit it is easier to take a shaving from the stile than to trim back a shoulder.

The rebated frame with a 'stuck' moulding (Fig 417) is in fact a simpler marking out, providing that the depth of

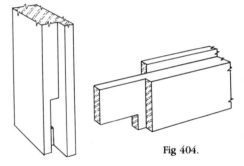

Fig 404.

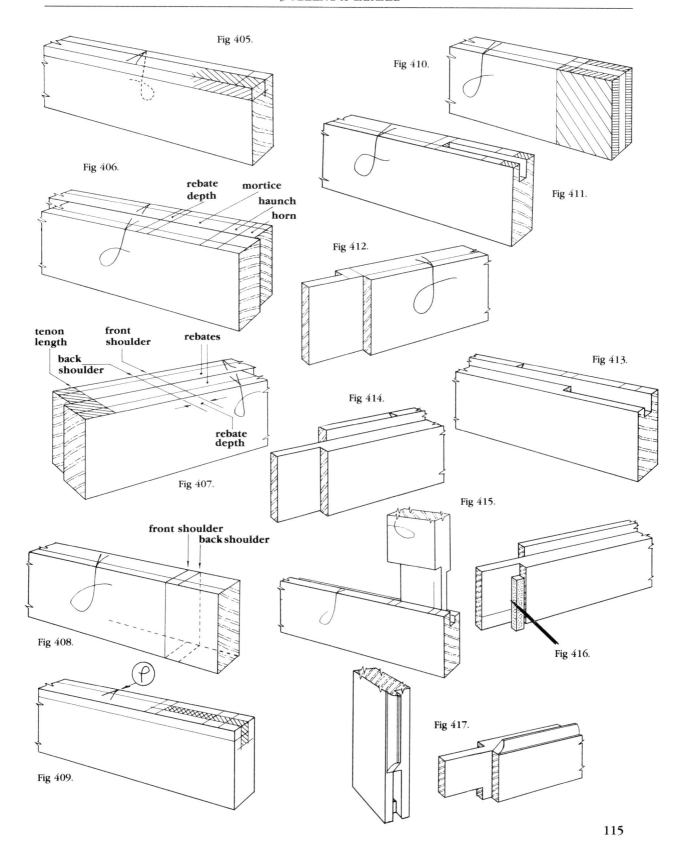

Fig 405.

Fig 410.

Fig 406.

rebate
depth

mortice

haunch

horn

Fig 411.

Fig 412.

tenon
length

front
shoulder

rebates

back
shoulder

Fig 413.

rebate
depth

Fig 414.

Fig 407.

Fig 415.

front shoulder
back shoulder

Fig 408.

Fig 416.

Fig 417.

Fig 409.

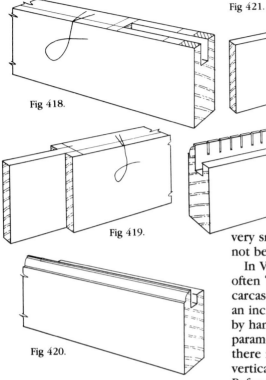

Fig 418.

Fig 419.

Fig 420.

Fig 421.

Fig 422.

Fig 423

Fig 424.

moulding is made the same as the depth of the rebate. Mark and cut stiles as Fig 418 and rails as Fig 419.

Work rebates and mouldings to give Figs 420 and 421 then cut the haunches. Remove the moulding on the stiles for the length of the mortice. Make a number of sawcuts across the moulding (Fig 422) then pare it away to the rebate level (Fig 423). Mitre all the moulding ends (Figs 424 and 402).

Fitting a door

The majority of doors are fitted flush and inside the carcase (Fig 425). This calls for a very well-made door and carcase, both free from twist, for errors of twist cannot be corrected. Alternatively the door may be slightly inset (Fig 426) or set slightly proud or outstanding (Fig 427). With these last two a

very small amount of twist will not be so noticeable.

In Victorian times doors were often 'planted' on the front of a carcase (Fig 428). There is now an increasing use of this method by hand craftsmen. It is of paramount importance that there is no twist across the vertical members of the carcase. Before the glue-up this must be

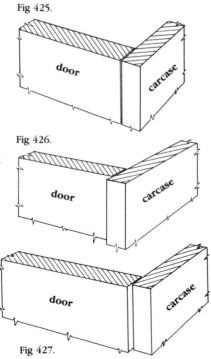

Fig 425.

Fig 426.

Fig 427.

carefully checked with the largest convenient winding strips.

This planted door has several advantages apart from a simpler fitting method. Fig 429 shows two identical glass-fronted cabinets, with the door set inside the carcase (A) and with the planted door (B). (Fitting the glass is dealt with at the end of the next chapter.) Both the door frames are of the same dimensions. The planted door has a comparatively lighter appearance. When a planted door is opened through 90° it moves clear of the carcase side (Fig 430). This is particularly useful in making possible the easy removal of the end volume of a row of books. A door fitted inside a carcase (Fig 431) requires 180° of movement, often not convenient, to give this facility.

In hanging an inside door (Fig 432) first fit the hingeing stile 1. Both carcase and stile should be straight, but if the carcase is a little out of true, plane the stile to fit. Having sawn off the horns the stiles will be marginally too long for the opening, but the fitting can still be accomplished. Next, plane the bottom edge, 2, to suit the angle of the carcase which should but may not quite be 90°. Then plane the top, *3*, to fit with two thicknesses of cartridge paper or very thin card under the bottom edge; this will give clearance to stop the door rasping. The bigger the door, the thicker the card. Finally, plane the closing edge, *4*. For comfortable opening this will eventually be angled slightly (Fig 433). The fitted door can be easily removed by inserting a screw in the eventual position of the knob, handle or keyhole.

The planted door is fitted in the same order. Where a top and bottom do not overhang, the closing edge can be finished after hingeing.

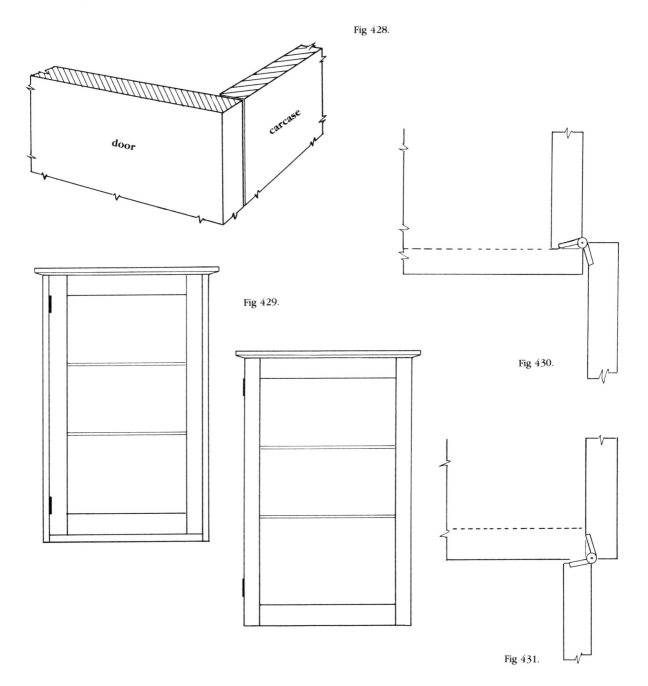

Fig 428.

Fig 429.

Fig 430.

Fig 431.

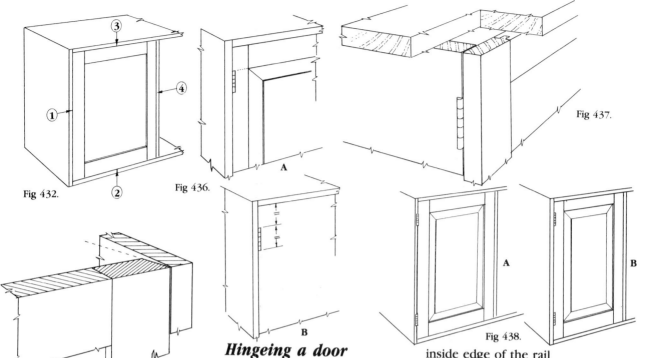

Fig 432.

Fig 436.

Fig 437.

Fig 438.

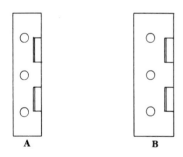

Fig 433.

Fig 434.

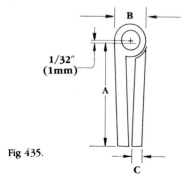

Fig 435.

Hingeing a door

The majority of doors are fitted with butt hinges (Fig 434)—for best-quality work they should be solid drawn brass not folded or merely plated. The illustration shows the two styles: the manufactured, broad suite (*B*) and the narrow suite (*A*), the second being more commonly used for furniture. The broad suite type is useful when a door is slightly outset, because in this case if a narrow suite hinge is used, the screws are liable to come too close to the carcase edge.

Three gauge settings will be used in the marking out (Fig 435, *A*, *B* and *C*). Three separate gauges, though not essential, save time and re-setting. Note that in setting *A* the gauge point should be just short of the hinge pin centre; 1mm (1/32in.) is about right.

The location of the hinges is important, particularly for their appearance. On a framed door the hinge lines up with the inside edge of the rail (Fig 436*A*). On a flush door the hinge is generally placed at its own length from the end (Fig 436*B*). The same rules apply to the hinges on a planted door (Fig 437). Hinges let into both door and carcase (Fig 438*A*) interrupt the straight line between door and carcase. In Fig 438*B* the hinge is let into the door only, preserving the continuous line, a more pleasing effect.

Mark the door first (Fig 439). The length is taken from the hinge itself and marked with a knife and square. Gauge the hinge width, *A*, on the edge and from the outside, i.e. the true face. Gauge the thickness, *B*, on the face. It is vital that this size is not exceeded otherwise the door will not close fully; if it is slightly undersize, the lesser evil, there will be a gap between the door and carcase which can be corrected. An overdeep socket will need packing up with veneer or card,

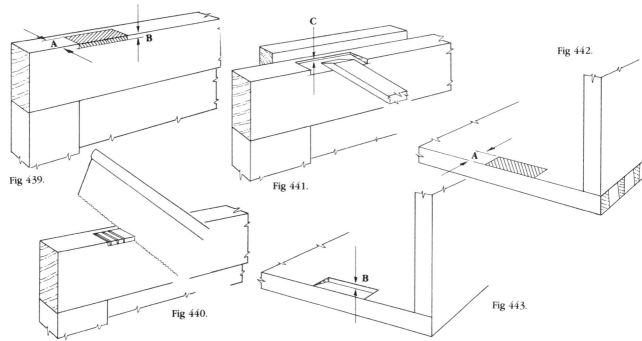

Fig 439.

Fig 441.

Fig 442.

Fig 440.

Fig 443.

or filling in and a fresh start, all unsightly.

The socket is formed by making a number of sawcuts (Fig 440) then removing the waste with a broad chisel (Fig 441). Notice that the socket reduces in depth towards the back where it finishes to a depth *C*, the thickness of the hinge leaf. Obviously this cannot be gauged, it must be found by trying the hinge. A socket too deep here will not affect the door closing but only its appearance. However the knuckle end is most critical as has already been mentioned. A block cramped to the door will prevent the chisel from accidentally bursting through.

Brass hinges need brass screws. With very hard woods it is easier to insert steel ones first, preferably *one* gauge smaller; these are replaced by brass when the hingeing is completed. Hinges sometimes need extra countersinking to ensure that the head does not

stand proud. Provisionally fit the hinges to the door with only one screw in place.

The door with its hinges is located in the carcase, standing on *one* thickness of the packing card. Mark the hinge position on the carcase and remove the door. Square these marks onto the inside and gauge the hinge width, *A* (Fig 442). Chop a chisel lightly across the grain in the manner of the sawcuts in Fig 440, remove the bulk of the waste and trim back the socket carefully to the lines. The maximum depth (Fig 443*B*) is the total hinge leaf thickness (Fig 435*B*). Again slight excess will not harm the fitting. *Nothing* must be removed at the carcase edge. Fix the hinge with one screw. Note that pilot holes for the screws must be drilled at right angles to the sloping bottoms of the sockets not to the face of the carcase.

Try the door for fit; a strip of thin paper should just pass down between the hinge stile

and the carcase. The closing stile may now need easing, at a slight angle. The odd shaving may still be needed elsewhere but with accurate marking and careful working this should be minimal.

For the best-quality work the hinges should now be unscrewed and rough scratches removed from the knuckles with successively finer grades of emery cloth, then metal polish. At the final screwing on, use brass screws and line up all their slots the same way.

If a stop is needed it can be made in the same manner as a drawer stop (see p.133).

Common faults when fitting doors are that either the door is 'screw bound' where protruding screw heads prevent the hinge from closing, or 'hinge bound' where the socket has been cut deeper than the total hinge thickness.

Fitting ball catches

The method most generally followed when fitting a ball catch (Fig 444) is to bore the door on the closing edge, either top or bottom. To eliminate wear, a brass striking plate is fitted to the carcase. This has a projecting tongue which is often too long and has to be filed back to fit. Generally this tongue is bent slightly for easy entry, making it necessary to cut into the carcase edge that little bit extra. The presence of this striking plate can mar the appearance of the door and a better alternative (assuming the carcase is thick enough) is to sink the ball catch into the carcase and fit the striking plate into the door so that nothing is visible (Fig 445). It can be done more often on a framed-up piece with square legs than on a dovetailed carcase.

As much of the polishing will have been done by this stage, strips of masking tape can be used to take the necessary marking. Close the door and mark across door and carcase. Open the door and square onto the inside edges. Gauge the centre of the door and with the same setting onto the carcase. Adjust where necessary for an inset or outset door (Fig 446).

Bore for the ball catch, first making a shallow hole for the flange then a deep hole for the barrel. Use a hand or machine dowel bit; an engineer's twist drill with its stubby point will not start accurately. Lay the striking plate on the marking and screw in place. Scribe round it, remove, cut out the necessary housing and replace. A shallow dimple can be drilled to take the ball. (Warning! If the knob or lock has not yet been fitted make sure that a small screw is temporarily fitted in that position otherwise the door will be extremely difficult to open.)

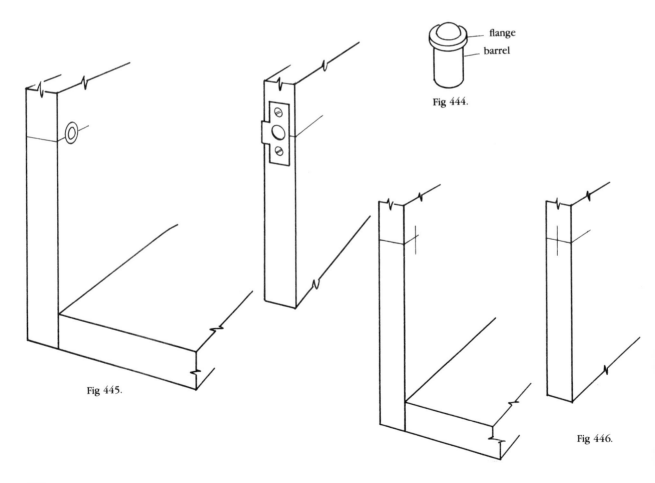

flange
barrel

Fig 444.

Fig 445.

Fig 446.

Fitting locks

The *straight* cupboard lock is screwed directly onto the inside of the door with no preparation, hence no description of the method is required. For quality work something better is required. This is the brass *cut lock* (Fig 447): 'cut' meaning cut into the door. The cut drawer lock is similar except that the keyhole is at right angles to that of the cupboard lock. In buying a cupboard lock specify whether it is to go into the right- or left-hand stile.

Prepare for marking by setting a marking gauge to the distance of the key pin (Fig 448). Mark the chosen position for the keyhole with a square on the face of the door then carry it round onto the edge. The gauge marks the distance from the edge (Fig 449). At this stage drill a very small pilot hole for the pin. Offer up the lock to the centre line and mark the length of the box on the door edge (Fig 450).

This is an essential method because on some locks the pin is by no means in the middle of the lock. Mark out this primary cavity with a square and gauge. Weaken the wood with a number of diagonal sawcuts. Waste can then be removed by chisel. Use the simple hand router to complete the process to depth (Fig 451).

Hold the lock in place and

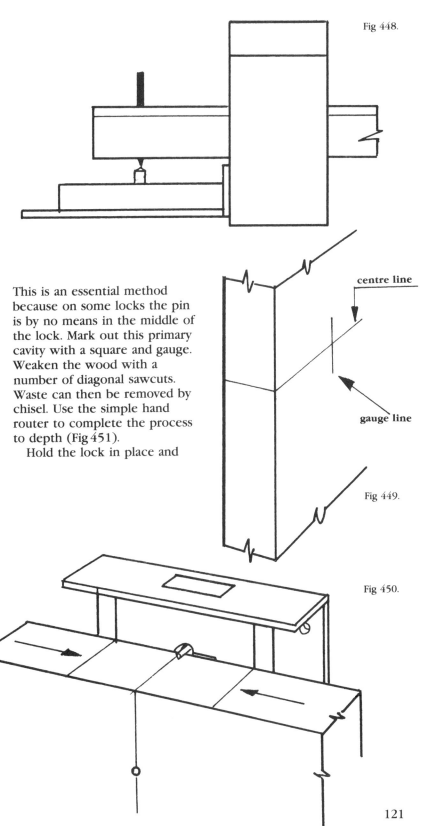

Fig 448.

centre line

gauge line

Fig 447.

Fig 449.

Fig 450.

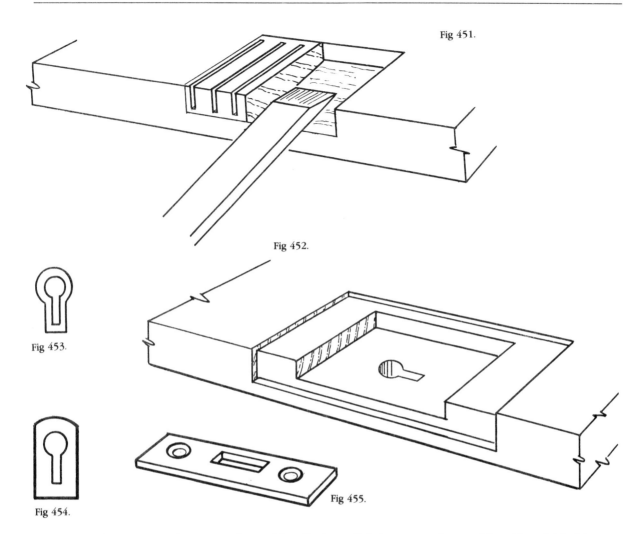

Fig 451.

Fig 452.

Fig 453.

Fig 454.

Fig 455.

scribe round it. Remove the waste to produce the second cavity (Fig 452). The keyhole can now be shaped using a larger drill and a coping saw. It may be finished with a round and a thin warding file. The keyhold is often left like this, but to prevent wear as the key is inserted an escutcheon may be fitted. The brass insert (Fig 453) requires the opening to be carefully filed out until the escutcheon can be pressed in with a G-cramp. Alternatively an escutcheon plate can be made from ebony, rosewood, bone, ivory, etc, and let into the door, either flush or slightly proud. A great variety of shapes is possible (e.g. Fig 454).

For fitting a drawer or *till lock* the routine is virtually the same. The socket for the bolt must be cut into the carcase. The door is closed with the bolt out, from which the length marking can be taken. Width markings can be made with a marking gauge (generally the points of a mortice gauge will not close sufficiently). Make due allowance for an inset or outset door. An alternative method favoured by some workers now is to ink the bolt end thoroughly with a thick felt marker and to quickly make a print with this before the ink dries, either onto the wood or onto a piece of masking tape. A brass plate can be recessed into the carcase to take the bolt. Unfortunately these are not usually for sale with the lock and must be individually hand made (Fig 455). (Making one by hand is an easy job—saw a piece of thin brass, file it to shape and drill holes in it for the screws.)

Cabinet bases

There is a considerable choice
of bases for cabinets, cupboards,
bookcases, chests of drawers
and similar pieces of furniture.
Fig 456 shows a typical stool
base. This is completely
straightforward, being the
standard table construction
already described. Generally the
stool is slightly projecting. A
simple moulding on the top
edge (Fig 457) blends the stool
and carcase together. An inset
stool, popular some years ago,

does not give such an
appearance of stability, nor does
it offer protection to the bottom
lap dovetails, always vulnerable
to brooms and cleaners
(Fig 458). Inset rails, polished
before the glue-up, speed up
the operation but do not blend
in easily when they stand
outside the carcase (Fig 459).
The box plinth (Fig 460) is an
old and well-tried base solution.
Traditionally the front corners
were secret mitre dovetailed.
This is not often done these

days, and is by no means a basic
skill. The rear corners are
generally lap dovetailed
(Fig 461).

The simplest front corner
joint is an accurately planed
mitre, glued (Fig 462) then
reinforced with a glued-in
corner fillet (Fig 463).
Additionally the mitre joint can
be strengthened with a plywood
tongue (Fig 464). This is not
really a hand process, but the
grooves can be cut on a small
sawbench or with a power

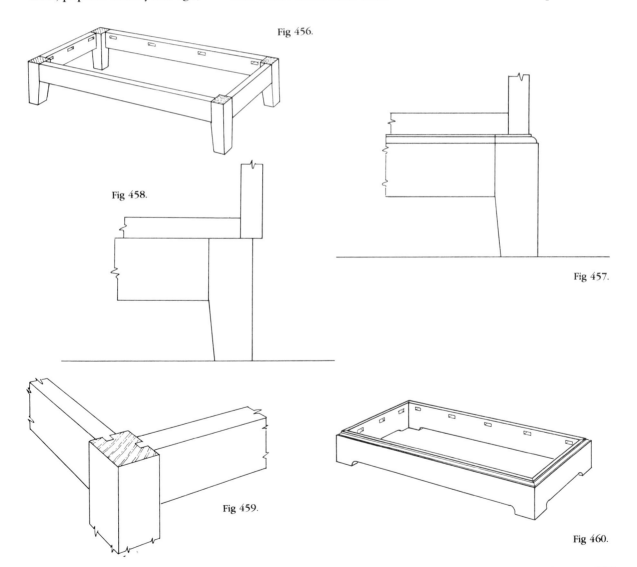

Fig 456.

Fig 458.

Fig 457.

Fig 459.

Fig 460.

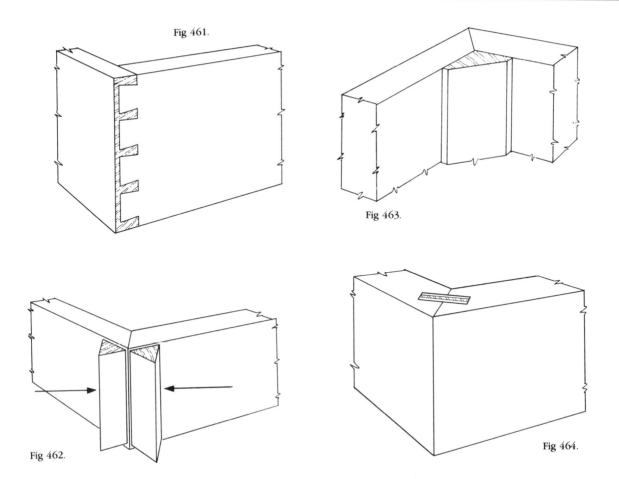

Fig 461.

Fig 463.

Fig 462.

Fig 464.

router with a simple 45° jig. Both these methods can also be used at the back.

On a cabinet given a chunky appearance, such as oak, elm or ash, the front corner of the plinth may be through dovetailed, and an alternative to this is the comb (or finger) joint; both are shown in Fig 465A and B. A number of machines provide facilities for cutting the comb joint but with a simple aid it can be cut on most sawbenches (Appendix G shows one such arrangement). Very wide comb joints present some difficulties in setting up. By hand, the comb joint is scarcely any easier to cut than

the common dovetail which certainly has more aesthetic appeal. A compromise between the two can be achieved by making a mitre and then strengthening it with triangular keys (Fig 466). A device for making the slots is given in Appendix F. Figure 467 shows a solution midway between stool and plinth, consisting of a morticed front block leg and a dovetailed back rail.

A carcase which has been given a heavy treatment can stand on block feet (Fig 468) and connecting rails are required for this. The front one may be through tenoned if other joints in the job are

through ones. Several shapes for the fronts are given (Fig 469). The back rail may still be lap dovetailed. Fig 470 shows block feet to which the cross rails are joined by half lap joints, their ends being treated decoratively.

Stools, plinths and block feet are all attached by means of shrinkage buttons (see p.75). The plinth can be left or cut away in one of a number of decorative forms as Fig 460 suggests. This treatment has the additional advantage in that it can, by providing four feet, reduce rocking on an uneven floor.

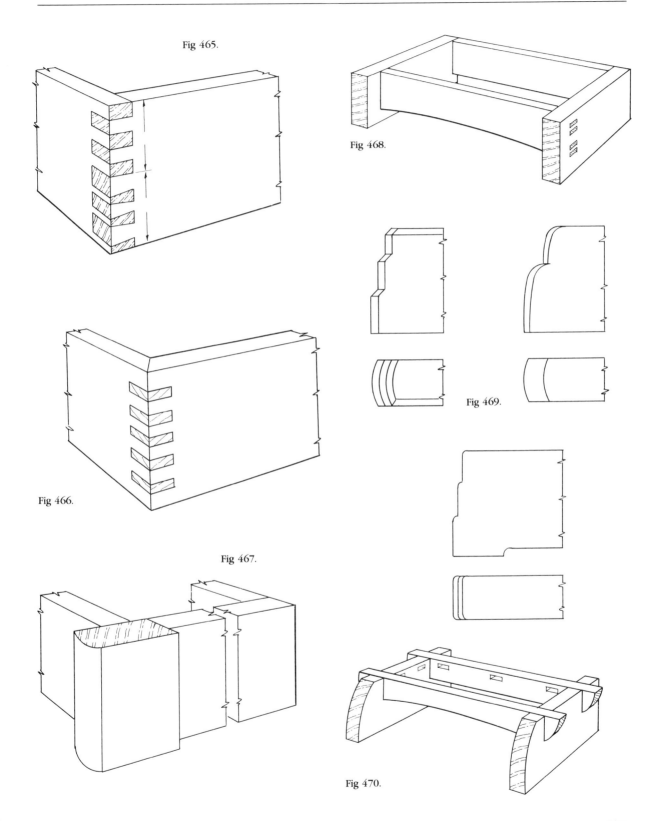

Fig 465.

Fig 468.

Fig 466.

Fig 469.

Fig 467.

Fig 470.

4 DRAWERS, HANDLES AND BOXES

Drawer making

A well-fitting drawer can be likened to a piston working in a cylinder. For a drawer to fit well, not only is it important that the drawer itself is absolutely accurate on the *outside*, but equally important is the accuracy of the opening into which it must slide. Therefore, when setting out a carcase, great care must be taken to see that the drawer opening is as large at the back of the job as it is at the front. Indeed, to ensure a really good fit, it is better to allow a very slight clearance at the back, both in height and in width. This will make certain that the drawer will not wedge at the back, and will allow for any slight inward bowing of the carcase.

The amount of this clearance is directly related to the length of the drawer side (Fig 471) but on the longest side should never exceed 1mm (1/32in.) on each side of the drawer; a greater amount would allow the drawer to wobble even when nearly closed. In the type of job where drawer guides are used, this clearance can easily be obtained (in width, but not in height) by adjusting the guides when the drawer is being fitted. Any twist in the carcase or framing will also cause a drawer to jam.

Test the accuracy of a job as it is being built. Take a small strip of wood about 3mm ($\frac{1}{8}$ in.) square, and cut it to length so that it just fits into the front of the opening into which the drawer will slide. Push it to the

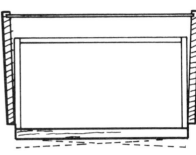

Fig 471.

Fig 471. Why a shallow drawer has greater side play than a deep one.

back where it should be a much slacker fit. This 'feeler gauge' test should be applied both horizontally and vertically, and should also be applied at the glueing stage when distortion caused by cramping may occur.

The joints Fig 472 shows the various joints used in drawer construction. The front joints are normal lap dovetails and, as they are exposed to view when the drawer is opened, they should be decorative as well as strong, with the pins not too large, say 3mm ($\frac{1}{8}$ in. thick at their thinnest point. It is the practice of some craftsmen to make this dimension as small as possible—in fact only the thickness of a fine dovetail saw. This causes the pins to appear 'floating' or detached from the rest of the front and so generally out of proportion with the rest of the joint.

The through dovetails at the back have a particular arrangement to allow for the fixing of the drawer bottom. The top edge of the back is set

down about 3mm ($\frac{1}{8}$ in.), and the bottom edge is raised so that the drawer bottom can be slid in beneath it. These spaces above and below the back allow the air to flow in and out as the drawer is moved. A larger space at the top would allow papers and other flat objects to fall over the back; 3mm ($\frac{1}{8}$ in.) clearance is ample.

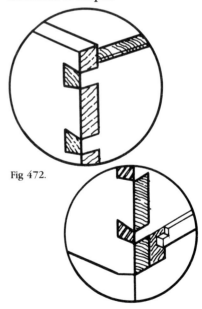

Fig 472.

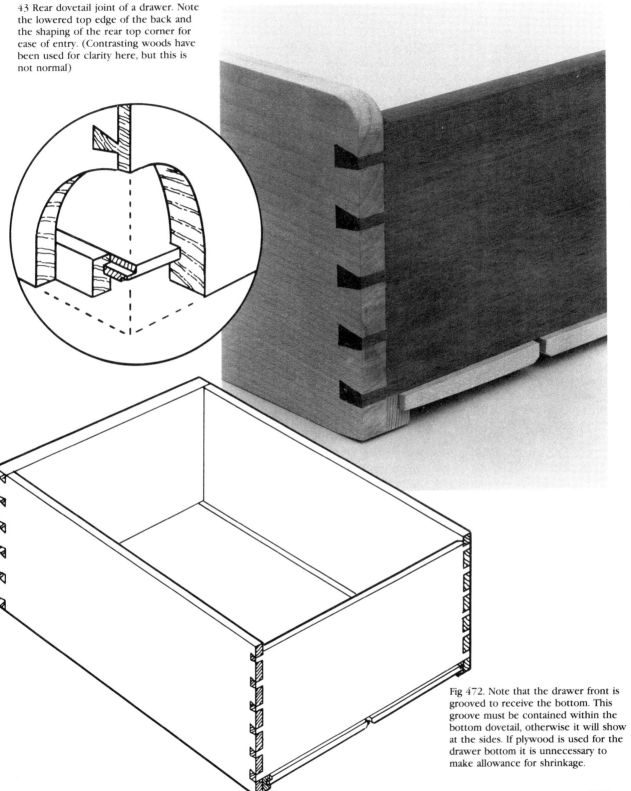

43 Rear dovetail joint of a drawer. Note the lowered top edge of the back and the shaping of the rear top corner for ease of entry. (Contrasting woods have been used for clarity here, but this is not normal)

Fig 472. Note that the drawer front is grooved to receive the bottom. This groove must be contained within the bottom dovetail, otherwise it will show at the sides. If plywood is used for the drawer bottom it is unnecessary to make allowance for shrinkage.

127

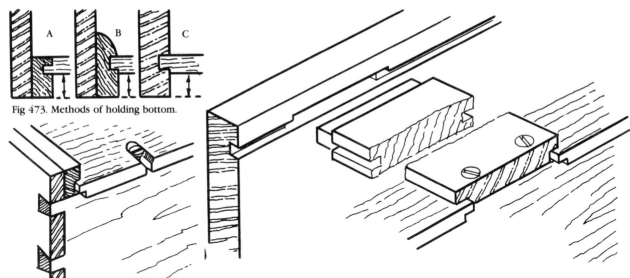

Fig 473. Methods of holding bottom.

Fig 474. Screw fixing of bottom to allow movement.

Fig 475. Muntin used for wide drawer.

Drawer bottom The method of fixing the drawer bottom to the side usually depends upon the material being used, or on the quality of job. Three commonly accepted methods are shown in Fig 473. Method *A* is used in the finest quality work, and with this method solid timber should be used for the bottom. If plywood were used, the top layer of veneer would be liable to chip along the shoulder. This method is suitable for desk drawers where papers and flat objects are housed. *B* is used in large drawers for housing linen, etc. It is somewhat stronger than *A* having a larger groove and is therefore capable of bearing more weight. Method *C* is simple and direct, but the absence of a drawer slip will cause the edge of the side to wear rapidly. This is usually countered by increasing the thickness of the side, but this gives the drawer a heavy, clumsy appearance. This method is used in carpentry, joinery and kitchen furniture.

The bottom has an important function in the construction of a drawer. Its front edge is tongued and glued into the drawer front so that the bottom will hold the whole drawer framework true and square (see inset Fig 472). It also keeps the sides straight, thus helping the drawer to run evenly. Where solid wood is used the grain should run from side to side of the drawer. The bottom must not be glued along the slips since allowance must be made for shrinking. To secure it along the rear edge the bottom is either slot screwed (solid wood) or screwed (plywood) to the underside of the drawer back (Fig 474). Where solid wood is used the back edge is left protruding about 3mm ($\frac{1}{8}$ in.). When the drawer is very large (e.g. in a chest of drawers) the bottom is not made of just one piece because this would tend to sag or split in the centre. It is divided into two, or even three parts, and muntins are fitted between them. These are like

very wide slips, except that they are not quite flush with the bottom edge of the drawer. They are morticed and tenoned into the drawer front and fastened up under the drawer back with screws (Fig 475).

Method of making
First mark the parts for their respective positions on the timber. Fig 476 shows the traditional marking, and allows for any number of drawers to be made at once without confusing the parts of the different drawers. The drawer sides should be arranged so that the direction of planing is as shown by the arrows. This will be a great help when the drawer is being fitted.

Drawer front Plane the inside of the drawer front true, testing for twist. This is important because a twisted front, being the thickest part, will cause the whole drawer to twist and it will not be able to run easily. Plane the bottom edge straight

Fig 476. Identification marks on parts.

and plough the groove to take the drawer bottom. Fit the front tightly, resting its bottom edge on the drawer rail. In a wide drawer the top edge can be left till later in case there is any shrinkage (Fig 477A).

Drawer back Plane the back to width and thickness and round the top edge. Fit it tightly into the front of the drawer opening, resting its bottom edge on the drawer rail. It will then be exactly the same length as the drawer front (Fig 477B).

Drawer sides Plane the sides to 1mm (1/32in.) more than the thickness required. It is essential to use a trying plane for this operation. No drawer will work easily if the sides are curved, and on the inside surface absolute flatness will facilitate the attachment of the slips. Next plane the bottom edges straight and fit the sides tightly in their respective positions (Fig 477C). Square off the sides to length so as to allow 13mm ($\frac{1}{2}$in.) clearance at the back of the drawer. It is advisable to bring the two sides together for this, so that their ends are identical. This will help to prevent the drawer being in twist.

Gauging Gauge the four pieces with a cutting gauge for the joints. When gauging the front and back for the thickness of the sides, set the gauge 1mm (1/32in.) *less* than the present thickness of the wood. The dovetails will, therefore, stand up 1mm (1/32in.) above the end grain of the pins, so that when this surplus thickness is planed off, the drawer will be

44 Nicely proportioned drawer dovetails

129

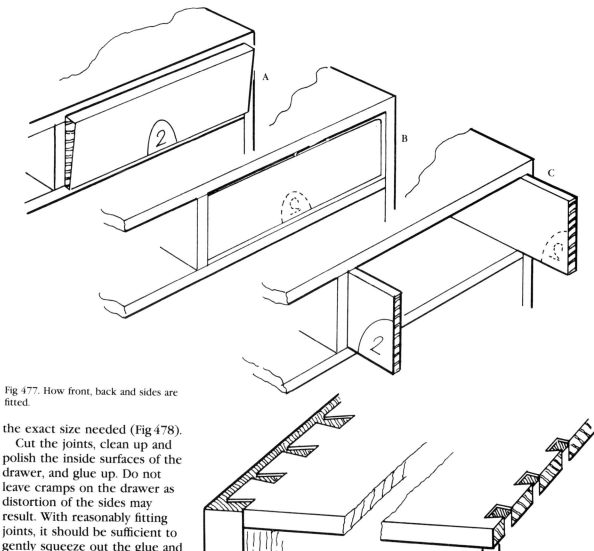

Fig 477. How front, back and sides are fitted.

the exact size needed (Fig 478).

Cut the joints, clean up and polish the inside surfaces of the drawer, and glue up. Do not leave cramps on the drawer as distortion of the sides may result. With reasonably fitting joints, it should be sufficient to gently squeeze out the glue and then remove the cramps. Check the whole for squareness and twist and leave to dry.

Drawer slips These usually present some difficulty to the beginner, being small and difficult to hold when ploughing the groove. They are much easier to make when a wide piece of wood is used. Plane the two edges straight, plough the necessary grooves, and then saw off the required width (Fig 479). When making type *B* in Fig 473, the quarter round should be

Fig 478. Dovetails standing proud, to allow for fitting.

worked before the slip is sawn off. A convenient method of making slips is to allow enough extra width on each drawer side for one slip. The groove is ploughed and the slip sawn off before the drawer side is fitted (see Fig 479). Attaching the slips to the drawer sides usually

presents difficulties to the beginner. Many cramps are needed, and cramping often causes the slip to slide out of position. If its jointing surface is planed once with a trying plane and the glue is hot and thin, the slip can be rub jointed.

To prevent the drawer slips

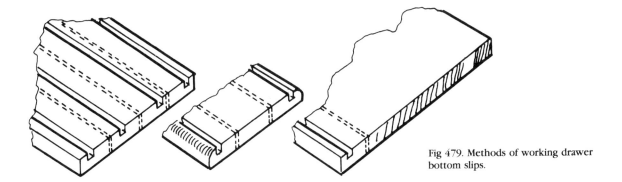

Fig 479. Methods of working drawer bottom slips.

from sliding when glueing in place, it is recommended that a tenon be cut on the front end, exactly the size of the groove. This locates in the groove in the drawer front (Fig 480*A* and *B*). The rear of the slip is notched to suit the drawer back (Fig 480*C*). In the case of Fig 473*A*, the slip is simply pushed firmly up against the drawer back.

Fitting the bottom Some difficulty may be experienced by the beginner in obtaining a good fit along the shoulders and in getting the bottom flush with the slips. An easy method is to fit the slips onto the bottom first, making the distance to the outside faces of the slips slightly greater than the inside size of the drawer (Fig 481). The slips are planed thinner until the whole fits exactly and then glued on to the drawer sides with the bottom removed.

Fitting the drawer First level off the bottom edges of the drawer. As the sides have already been fitted into the carcase, only *very little* should be removed from their edges. Then remove the extra thickness allowed on the drawer sides. For the drawer to fit evenly throughout its

movement, it is *absolutely essential* for the sides to be straight and flat. To achieve this use a trying plane and support each side whilst it is being planed or it will bend under the pressure of the plane. Fig 482 shows the method of holding

the drawer whilst providing this support. To prevent chipping the end grain of the drawer front, the direction of planing should be away from the front dovetails, but planing in this direction often results in the back of the drawer being made

Fig 480.

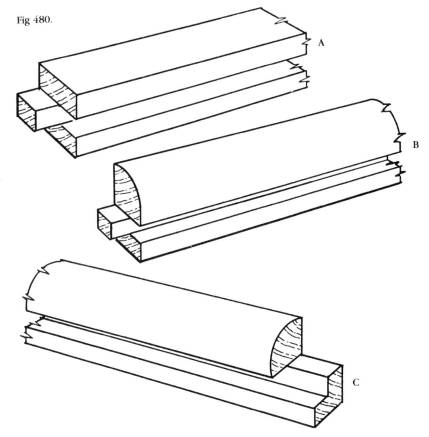

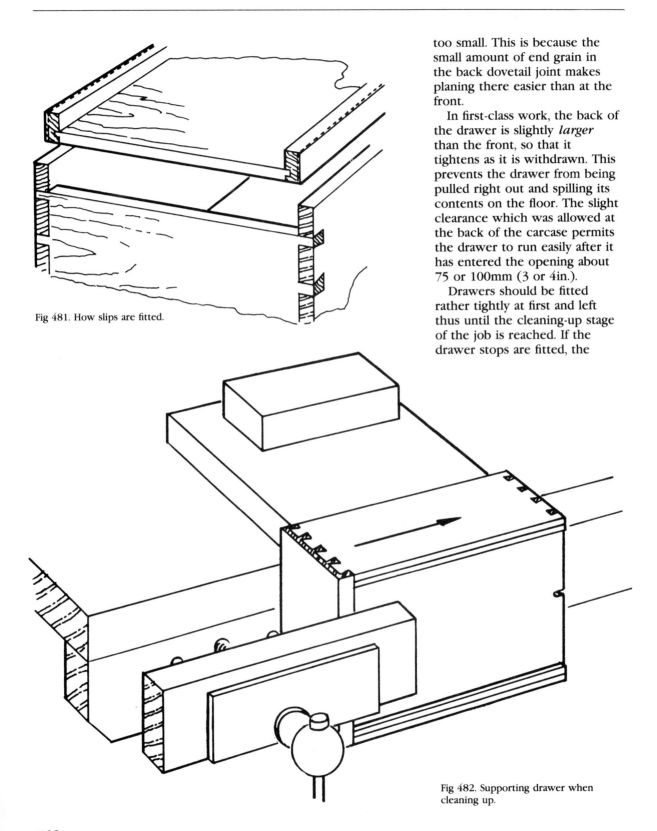

Fig 481. How slips are fitted.

too small. This is because the small amount of end grain in the back dovetail joint makes planing there easier than at the front.

In first-class work, the back of the drawer is slightly *larger* than the front, so that it tightens as it is withdrawn. This prevents the drawer from being pulled right out and spilling its contents on the floor. The slight clearance which was allowed at the back of the carcase permits the drawer to run easily after it has entered the opening about 75 or 100mm (3 or 4in.).

Drawers should be fitted rather tightly at first and left thus until the cleaning-up stage of the job is reached. If the drawer stops are fitted, the

Fig 482. Supporting drawer when cleaning up.

Fig 483. Best form of drawer stop.

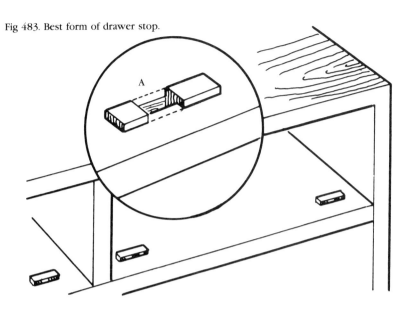

use is Ronuk floor wax, as it is not sticky and is easily applied. The common practice of using paraffin wax has the disadvantage that glasspaper is needed afterwards to remove—and spread—the surplus wax, and the grit from the glasspaper tends to become embedded in the drawer sides and elsewhere. This can easily cause the familiar scratches and grooves which often appear on the sides and bottom edges of drawers.

Scotch glue is less frequently used now, and modern PVA and synthetic glues do not lend themselves to the rubbed joint technique, so the drawer slips need to be cramped. To obviate the excessive weight of iron cramps, it is worth making for this purpose eight or ten light wood cramps (see Appendix H).

front can be planed flush or parallel with the face of the job. Fig 483A shows the best type of stop to use, and by planing its front edge before it is glued in, the position of the drawer can

be adjusted should the thickness of the front vary.

Finishing When the drawer has had its final fitting, lubricate the parts which are subjected to friction. The best material to

45 Glueing in drawer slip with workshop-made cramps. These are a tiny fraction of the weight of iron cramps

Drawer framing

In the solid wood or carcase construction, drawers are supported at the front by the drawer rail (Fig 483). This is both tenoned and housed into the cabinet side (Fig 484). A similar rail can be fitted at the back, although this is sometimes omitted, particularly when the back is sufficient to keep the cabinet rigid. In the best work, dust panels are fitted between the drawers. Drawer rails and other components are grooved to accept these, which means that a rear drawer rail is essential.

The drawer rails are connected by the drawer bearers, also housed but not glued into the sides. At the front the bearer is tenoned into the drawer rail (Fig 484) and this joint is glued. At the rear, as shown in Fig 483, the shoulder is cut back, the mortice made deeper and the joint not glued. This permits the cabinet side to expand or contract without splitting or warping, the bearer remaining in place whatever happens.

In small cabinets or where it has been chosen to omit the rear drawer rails, the bearer is arranged as in Fig 485. The front end is tenoned and glued into the drawer rail. It is housed, but not glued to the side. The rear end is cut away and secured by a round-head screw in a slot, thus permitting movement of the side (Fig 486).

A framed and panelled cabinet requires different treatment (Fig 487). The front and rear drawer rails are tenoned and housed into the leg or corner member (Fig 488). The drawer bearer is tenoned into both rails. These joints are glued, but

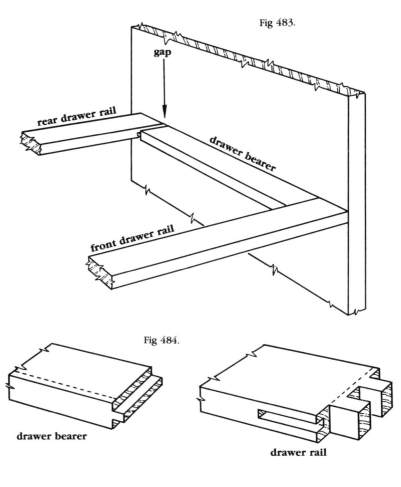

Fig 483.

gap

rear drawer rail

drawer bearer

front drawer rail

Fig 484.

drawer bearer

drawer rail

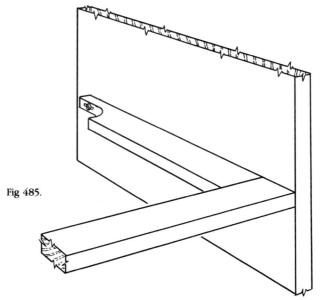

Fig 485.

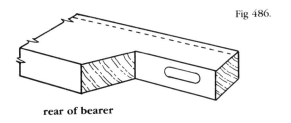

Fig 486.

rear of bearer

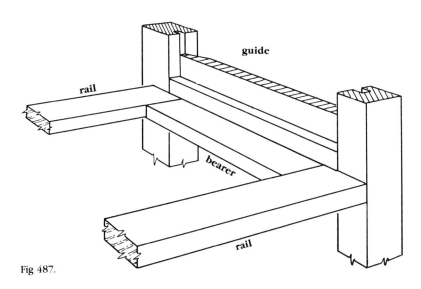

guide

rail

bearer

rail

Fig 487.

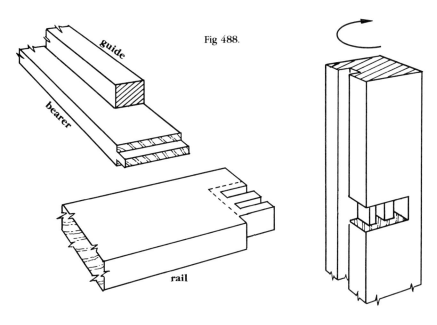

guide

bearer

Fig 488.

rail

the bearer must not be glued to the panel. At one time guides were housed into the bearers but now a simple glue joint is considered adequate. Where the back drawer rail is omitted the arrangement of Fig 488 is used, housing the end round the corner member. The guide is glued on as before.

Note that while front drawer rails are generally flush with the sides, at the rear provision must be made for the groove or rebate, cut later, accommodating the cabinet back.

Handles

Wooden handles, apart from those manufactured commercially, fall into two categories, turned and bench made. There is no great distinction between those for drawers and those for doors.

In Fig 489, *a* shows the quickest, easiest and cheapest form, often found on modern mass produced furniture. A length of material is machined to section then sawn off in length. It is seldom produced by hand using moulding planes, but can quickly be made with a power router. Such handles are fixed, generally horizontally, by two screws from the inside of the drawer. *Screwed-on handles*, possibly in more exotic woods, in forms similar to *b* are an improvement.

Quality handles, in woods such as rosewood and ebony, *c*, are tenoned into the door or drawer. If the tenon is brought through it can be wedged. These handles show end grain on the front; this polishes well to give a most attractive appearance, but if the tenon is

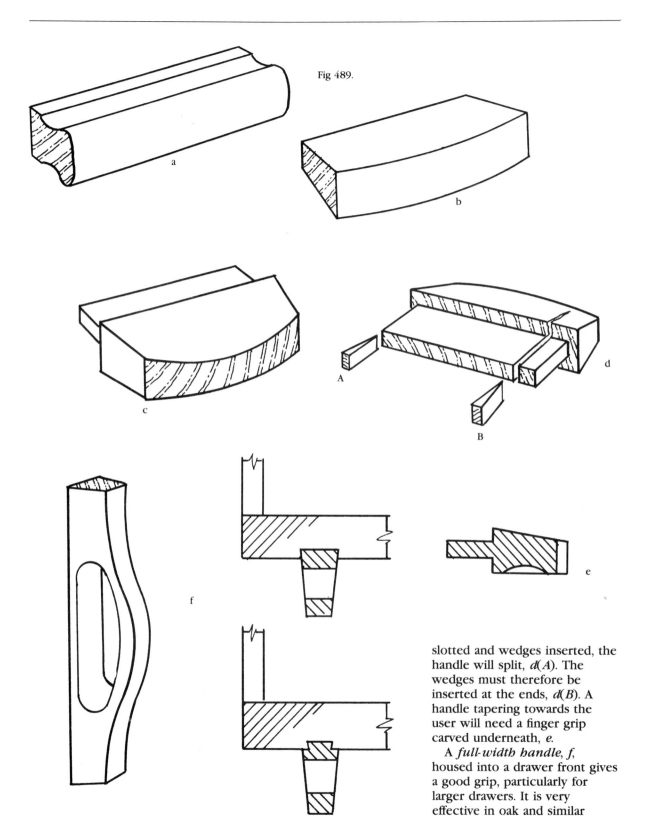

Fig 489.

slotted and wedges inserted, the handle will split, *d*(*A*). The wedges must therefore be inserted at the ends, *d*(*B*). A handle tapering towards the user will need a finger grip carved underneath, *e*.

A *full-width handle*, *f*, housed into a drawer front gives a good grip, particularly for larger drawers. It is very effective in oak and similar

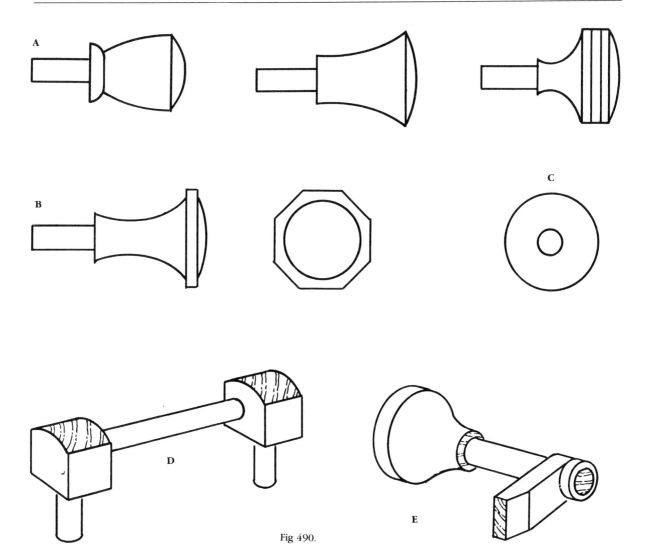

Fig 490.

woods, and where a number of drawers is stacked vertically as in a chest of drawers. The dovetail housing can be stopped just short of the top edge of the drawer.

Turned handles (Fig 490) always present end grain to the viewer, so the finish on this face must be immaculate to exploit its appearance to the full. Although these handles may be screwed from the inside, they tend to work loose and rotate; very little extra effort is required to turn a small tenon and to bore the drawer front for it, and you will be happier with the result. Set a caliper to the drill and turn to this size. Unless you are working with small pieces of exotic woods, a number of handles are turned together between centres and then parted off. The face is finished off finely by gripping the tenon either in a wood chuck or in a drill chuck. A great variety of shapes is possible and those in Fig 490A, are typical. By careful paring or disc sanding, polygonal features can be introduced, *B*. An inlaid central contrasting dot can be added, e.g. sycamore or holly in ebony, *C*. Turning and bench work can combine to give bar handles, *D*, in which the use of contrasting woods may be effective. This style does not appear to be used in the vertical form. In oak or similar chunky woods a rotating latch can be arranged, *E*.

Box constructions

Boxes vary greatly in size from small jewellery cases to tool boxes which are virtually carcases, and there is a range of jointing methods.

The simplest, the *nailed butt joint*, is used only for crude or temporary work (Fig 491). A refinement (Fig 492) gives a shoulder which helps to keep the components square and also reduces the amount of end grain visible. It can be pinned or strengthened with *feathers* of veneer (see below). Both these joints are fundamentally unsound since at every glueing point one of the components is end grain, which has no glueing strength.

A *mitre joint* (Fig 493) giving half end grain glueing surfaces though slightly stronger is suitable, unstrengthened, only for small jobs. Although the mitres can be cut on the circular saw, they will need to be finished by hand planing on an accurate mitre shooting board. The strength of this joint can be improved by the addition of a loose tongue (Fig 494). The grooves for this are generally cut by radial arm saw, or else using suitable jigs on the circular saw or router table. Alternatively a router may be used with a thick 45° block (see Appendices C and D.) Note that to obtain a good size of tongue, the groove is not central but is set inwards of centre. Tongues should be of plywood or, if visible, of cross grain hardwood. A modern innovation is the 'biscuit jointer' which cuts slots into which are glued elliptical tongues of compressed beech, but this method is only suitable for the larger sizes.

The mitred joint can be

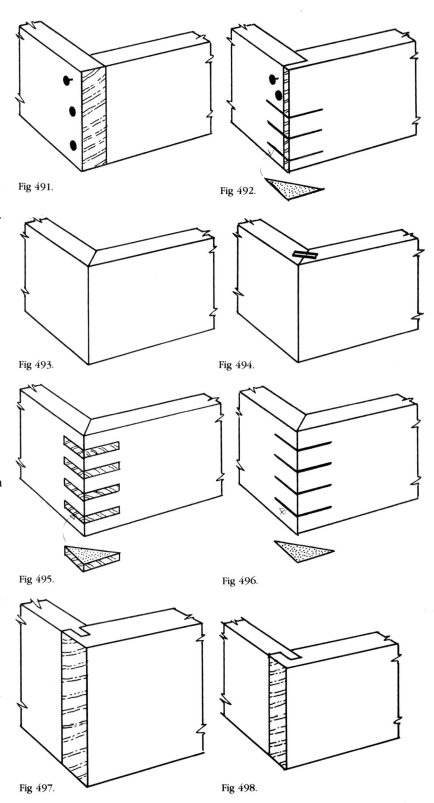

Fig 491.

Fig 492.

Fig 493.

Fig 494.

Fig 495.

Fig 496.

Fig 497.

Fig 498.

138

46 The keyed mitre joint. Stronger than mere veneer keys and producing a decorative effect

strengthened by *feathers*. On small work a piece of veneer or even two thicknesses can be used (Fig 496). The problem generally met with here is to match up veneer and saw thickness. Sawcuts are sometimes made dovetail fashion. Larger work can be given feathers of solid wood (Fig 495) in thicknesses between 2 and 4mm (1/16 and 3/16in.). The joints are glued, cleaned up and carefully handled during the slotting. The slotting is easily done on a small overhead router, using the appropriate slotting cutter and a 'vee' fence into which the box is fed. Alternatively, if the box is not too large, the sawbench can be used, perhaps with wobble washers to adjust the width of the cut. A suitable cradle is shown in Appendix F.

With small circular saws and routers various *interlocking corner joints* are possible. Two of these, popular for small, commercially made boxes, are given in Figs 497 and 498.

The *comb* or *finger joint* (Fig 499) can be, though seldom is, cut by hand. Industrial scale machines exist for this joint but it can easily be arranged on a small sawbench. Wobble washers increase the width of the sawcut, which for the best appearance should not exceed 6mm ($\frac{1}{4}$in.). Many sawbenches have an attachment for cutting this joint. Appendix G shows a simply made jig which can easily be adapted to work on a router table also. By bypassing the register pin it is possible to arrange a mitred corner.

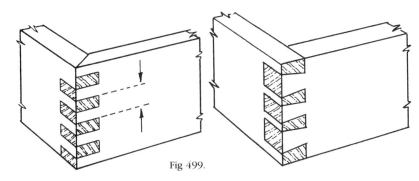

Fig 499.

139

Generally the spacing is planned as accurately as possible but the final height of the box must be in multiples of the joint. Sawing through the box to provide the lid necessitates the removal of one complete unit to preserve the pattern.

The making of the *dovetail joint* (Fig 500) has already been dealt with. It is the commonest joint for quality boxes. The dovetails are on the front of the box and the tails on the ends. Generally the top and bottom corners are mitred to take the groove fixing the top and bottom of the box, although nowadays grooving with the power router no longer renders this essential. Where there is a sawn-off lid, one dovetail is made extra wide to allow for the loss in sawing and planing (Fig 501). Where the thickness of the sides reduces, giving a sloping-sided box, it is customary to match this by diminishing the dovetails (Fig 502, see also Appendix I).

Box bottoms can be grooved in, rebated or rebated with a slip (Fig 503*A*, *B*, *C* and *D*). Veneered ply can be glued in but solid wood must be left free to move, as in *A*, *C* or *D*.

A planted top (Fig 504) presents no difficulties but problems can arise with the sawn-off type unless quarter sawn wood is very carefully chosen. A grooved-in top (Fig 505*A*) may warp, distorting its frame and producing the effects of Fig 506. A thinner top, built up as in Fig 505*B* is less likely to warp, and *C* still less. These extra slips should be cut from the sides and ends of the

47 The comb or finger joint. Easily jigged on the sawbench

Fig 501.

140

top material and be butt jointed, not mitred at the corners. A bevel or cove softens the inside corner (Fig 507).

Fig 508 shows an alternative top construction. Veneered plywood is glued into a rebate and the joint concealed with inlay stringing.

To assist in closing a box accurately and provide some measure of dustproofing and airtightness, loose linings are added to good-quality boxes, often in contrasting woods (Fig 509). These should be kept as thin as possible 3mm ($\frac{1}{8}$ in.) is a common thickness) and are mitred at the corners. They are not generally glued in and the top edges are often half-rounded. The front liner will need to be planed back at a minute angle to permit the lid to close easily. A step on the liner provides the support for a tray.

A small bead, possibly of the same wood as the linings, is sometimes mitred and glued to the edge of the lid (Fig 510). This may be swelled out at the middle of the front to give a finger grip for opening. Care must be exercised at the back to blend in with the hinges. For this reason the back is sometimes left flush.

When veneer is laid over corner joints they always show through eventually. This reduces the choice of corner joints in the veneered box to a plain mitre, a mitre with tongue, or a mitre with veneer feathers.

A completely different method of box-making is shown in Figs 511A and B. Two sides are extended beyond the box. This form may be joined by dowelling, through (C) or concealed, mortice and tenon,

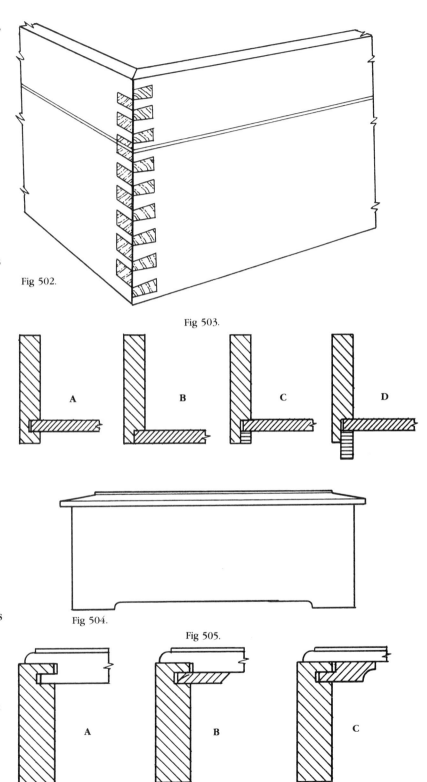

Fig 502.

Fig 503.

A   B   C   D

Fig 504.

Fig 505.

A   B   C

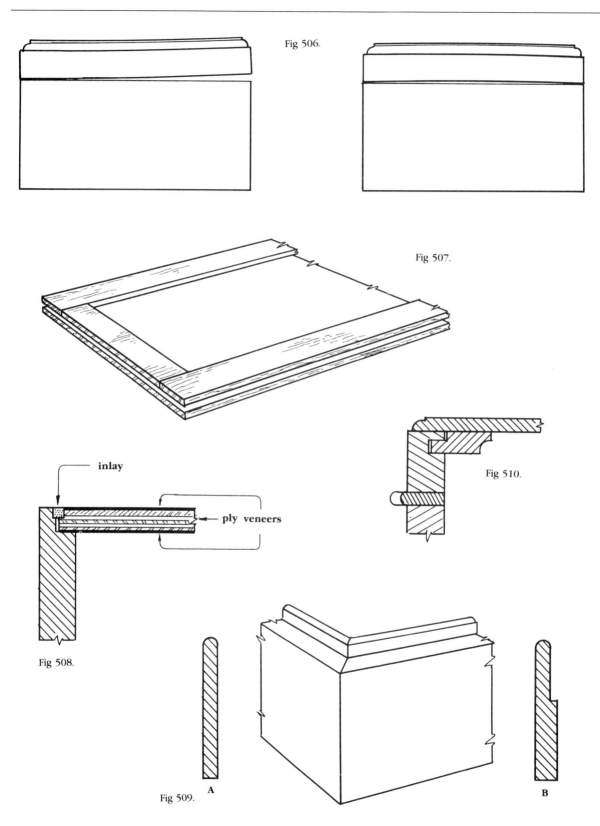

Fig 506.

Fig 507.

inlay

ply veneers

Fig 510.

Fig 508.

Fig 509.   A

B

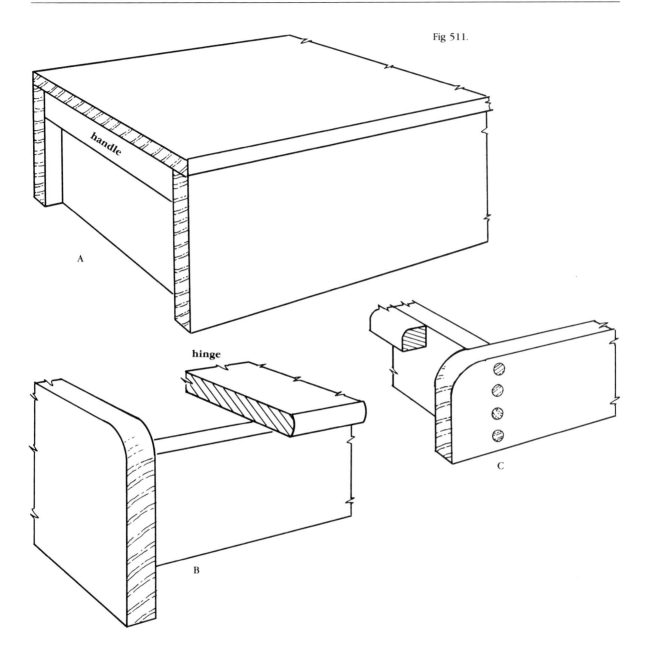

Fig 511.

through or stopped, or by dovetailed housing. Where the front and back project the opportunity can be taken to incorporate a handle strip (as in *A*). Where the ends project, the hinged lid can overlap (*B*) to form a finger grip.

A simple method of glueing up is shown in Appendix E.

Box hingeing

On small boxes the hinges are generally let in equally to the box and the lid (Fig 512). Where a lipping or cocked bead has been used, it should be made the same thickness as the hinge, which is then completely let into this member (Fig 513). In this case, the other lap of the

hinge is let into a tapered socket (Fig 514) in the manner of door hingeing.

Small boxes with light lids can be hinged (Figs 515 and 516). The small bevels planed along the back edges of the lid and the box permit the lid to support itself when fully open. On a larger box the leverage

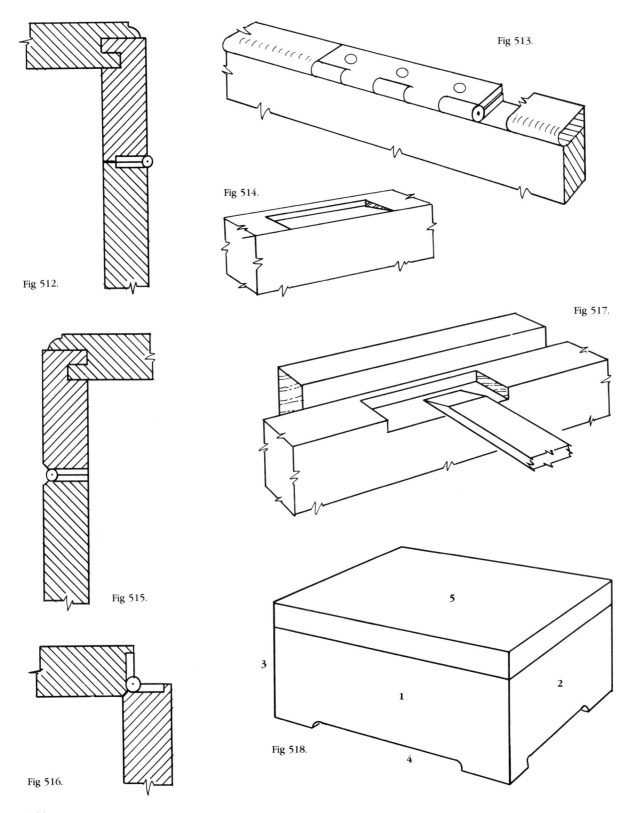

Fig 512.

Fig 513.

Fig 514.

Fig 515.

Fig 516.

Fig 517.

Fig 518.

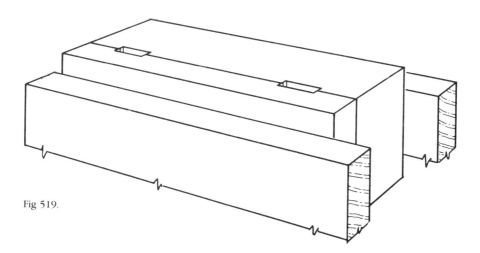

Fig 519.

will be too great and the screws will be torn out. Remember to use a supporting block when cutting out the housings (Fig 517).

When the hingeing is complete skim and clean up the faces in the order shown (Fig 518) (note that the hinge face is omitted). Bottom and top follow if they are flush. An inset bottom or a raised top must be polished before the glue-up.

Remove the hinges (Fig 519) and carefully re-assemble the box. Position the box and lid very carefully and hold them in place with masking tape. The hinge face can now be finished and the hinges returned.

Glass and mirrors

The treatment of glass and mirrors will vary according to the quality of the job. The most common method of constructing glazed panels and doors has already been touched upon (see pp.108 and 114). Figure 520 is a typical section. An ovolo mould or bevel is worked on the outside with a rebate, generally of the same depth as the moulding, on the inside. Pin (don't glue) a small

bead, either flush or round-nosed, on the inside. This permits easy replacement of the glass. Brass pins or small brass screws look better than steel and will not rust. However, as timbers shrink, particularly in a centrally heated room, this method can result in rattling panels.

This problem can be reduced by bedding the glass in a very thin layer of putty. If the work is not to be painted, putty of a suitable colour must be chosen

or else a powder colour must be mixed with white putty. Paint the inside of the rebate to prevent the linseed oil in the putty from leaching through. In very thin frames the glass can be secured by putty alone on the inside (Fig 521). This was often done on period pieces. A few pins hold the glass in place, to be concealed by the putty. Again, paint the rebate and choose a suitable colour for the putty.

Mirrors can be similarly

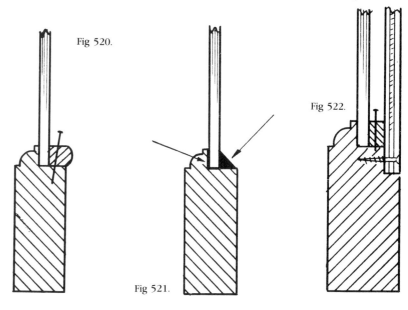

Fig 520.

Fig 522.

Fig 521.

secured. To prevent unpleasant reflections, give the rebates and the edges of the mirror a coat of matt black (blackboard) paint. There should be an air space between mirror and backing. In a thick frame or door this can be carried out as shown in Fig 522. The ply backing can be merely planted on but a neater job is made if it is screwed into a second rebate. With smaller mirrors the classic method is to secure the mirror into its rebate by means of small softwood wedges glued to the frame (Fig 523). The glass should be about 1.5mm (1/16in.) undersize all round. In the best work the mirror is bedded in a very thin layer of putty. This compensates for any slight twist, particularly in circular or polygonal frames. This method gives a good bed for bevelled glass (Fig 524A).

Figure 524B shows how a mirror frame may be built up, the joints being concealed by mouldings or inlay. Figure 524C gives an alternative where the front facing is built up from one or two thicknesses of sawcut veneer. This method, using cross grained veneer was commonly used on period pieces.

Having described traditional treatments, it is a fact that modern silvering is much more robust than earlier methods. This is borne out by the popularity of mirror tiles, attached by means of adhesive foam pads. Fig 525 shows an easier and quicker method which has proved successful over a number of years with modern mirrors. A number of small foam pads are compressed between the backing and the mirror, holding the latter firmly in place.

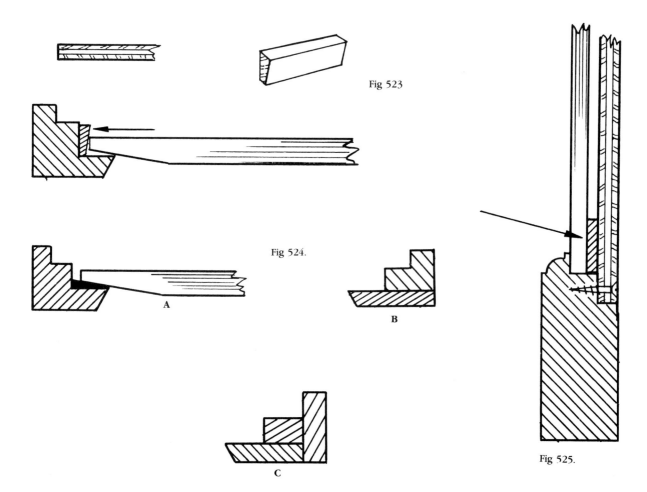

Fig 523

Fig 524.

A

B

C

Fig 525.

APPENDIX A

Sawing boards

These can be made from any offcuts, preferably of hardwoods. The stops are ideally glued and dowelled as screws tend to work loose.

Type *A* is the common double-sided type, of which one stop may be gripped in the bench vice. The sawing is then done across the bench. Type *B* shows a less common form, particularly useful for beginners. The under block must be held in the vice, so sawing is along the length of the bench, as is planing. This permits the work to be held firm with a G-cramp or handscrew.

It is worth making both. Type *A* is most useful for long pieces, in which case it is helpful to have a second similar one, possibly narrower, to hold the long piece firm and level.

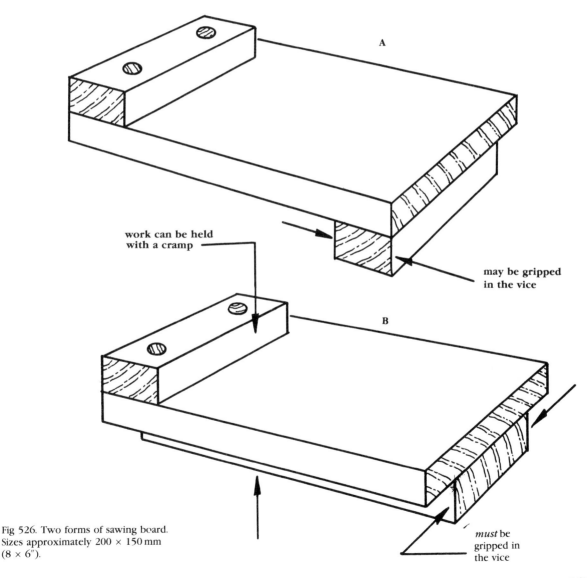

A

work can be held with a cramp

may be gripped in the vice

B

Fig 526. Two forms of sawing board. Sizes approximately 200 × 150 mm (8 × 6″).

must be gripped in the vice

APPENDIX B

The rip tenon saw

In sawing tenon cheeks, the longer the saw stays in the sawcut, the greater the risk of inaccuracy, so it must be very sharp. An improvement is to have a tenon saw re-cut, removing its crosscut teeth, generally about 15 teeth per 25mm (1in.) and replacing these by ripsaw teeth, 10 teeth per 25mm (1in.). The teeth can easily be spaced by cramping to the saw an old power hacksaw blade of 9 or 10tpi. The greater speed of the ripsaw gives an improvement to accuracy and a reduction in effort. An added advantage is that 10tpi can be set using the common pliers-type sawset, which will not operate on more than 12tpi. Re-cutting can be let out to a saw sharpening firm.

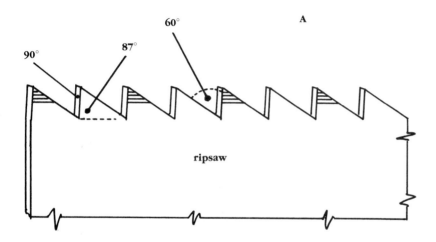

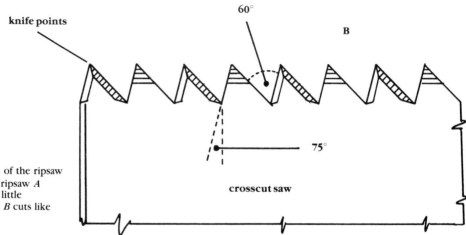

Fig 527. Showing the teeth of the ripsaw and the crosscut saw. The ripsaw *A* cuts like chisels, removing little shavings. The crosscut saw *B* cuts like knives, removing dust.

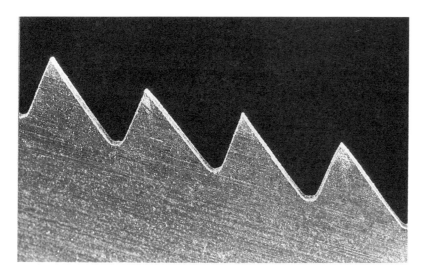

48 The ripsaw—shaped and sharpened

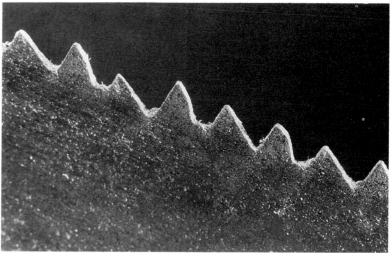

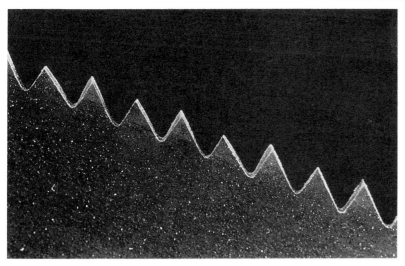

50 Crosscut handsaw—teeth shaped and sharpened

APPENDIX C

An aid to groove mitre joints by router

A thick block of well-seasoned material (or a built-up piece) is carefully planed at 45°. With great accuracy the acute angle is planed back to 90° from the 45° face to accept the router's fence. The workpiece is cramped to this, the block held by its edges in a large vice and the groove routed out (Fig 528).

Fig 528.

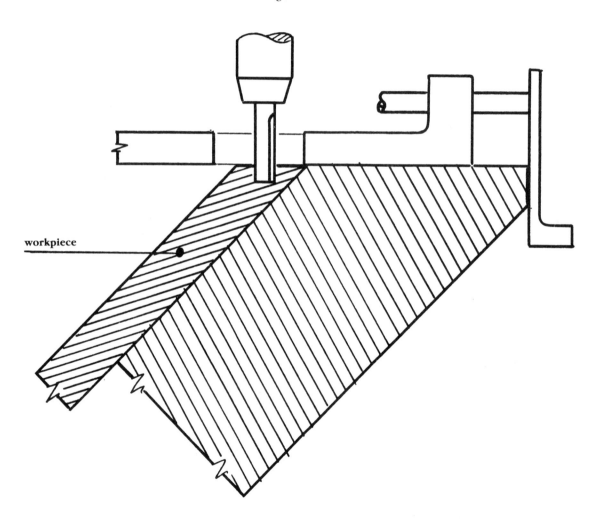

workpiece

APPENDIX D

An aid to groove mitre joints on the circular saw

Only multi-ply should be used; solid wood may shrink or expand, affecting the accuracy of the 45° angle.

The baseplate *A* and the working face *B* are jointed at 45°. The real accuracy is provided by the two angle blocks *C*. The base *A* and sub-base *D* are both identically grooved to take two metal or wood strips, *G*. These are screwed to *D*, allowing *A* to slide along them. A bolt, washer and wing-nut *H* in a slot in *A* allows the work to be positioned precisely over the saw.

A metal bar *I* is fitted beneath *D* to match the groove in the sawbench. This bar is screwed from above. The two screws *J* operate through oversize holes in *D*. This allows adjustment so that the working face *B* is precisely parallel to the sawblade.

A handle *F* is fitted between the two angle blocks *C*.

A thin fence strip, *E*, is screwed vertically to the workface in a position convenient for the width of the material being handled. Check with a large setsquare against the saw table. This piece both aligns and pushes the work forward, so accuracy of fixing is important.

The work must be held firm with a small G-cramp. Sizes will depend on the particular sawbench and the width of joints. Remember to use suitable guarding.

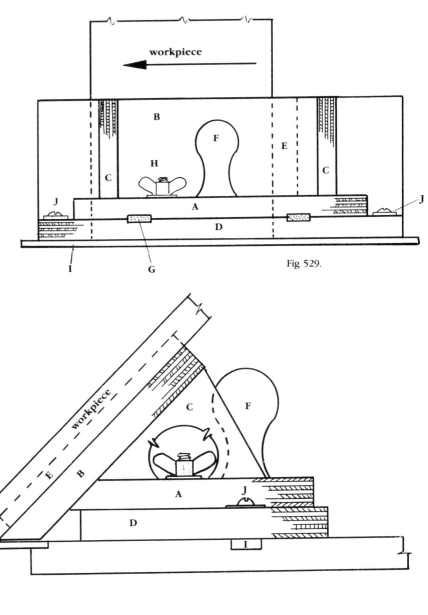

Fig 529.

Fig 530.

APPENDIX E

Glueing up mitred boxes

Boxes can most conveniently be glued up in the following manner. Machine a length of material for the four corner blocks. The rebate is most easily taken out by circular saw. Arrange a cut slightly deeper than the required rebate, which gives a clearance in the corner. Round the external corner and sand smooth, then cut into lengths. Either wax the pressure faces or cover with plastic tape to prevent surplus glue from adhering to them (*A*). Assemble as in *B*. Apply pressure for smaller boxes with strong rubber bands (e.g. cut from motor car inner tubes) or for larger sizes with a commercial web cramp.

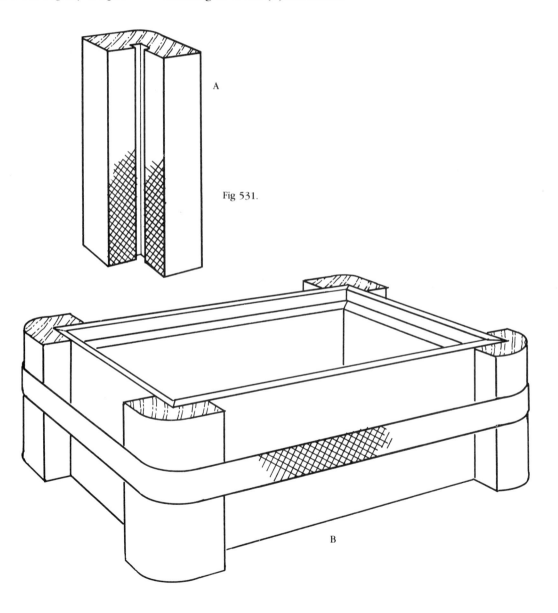

A

Fig 531.

B

APPENDIX F

An aid to make keyed mitre joints

Components *A* and *B* are glue jointed together to form a cradle which holds the box. Before glueing, cut two 6mm ($\frac{1}{4}$in.) slots in *B*.

The cradle is notched then secured to the two runners, *C*, reinforced by four accurately formed 45° blocks, *D*. Check that the resultant angle is 90°. Obtain a piece of metal bar to suit the sawbench groove. Drill and tap this 6mm ($\frac{1}{4}$in.). The bar is secured to one of the runners, *C*, by two screws with washers, *G*. These screws, operating in oversize holes, permit accurate adjustment of the cradle which must be at right angles to both the circular saw and the bar *F*.

A moving fence, *E*, is held in the cradle, secured to *B* either by round, headed screws with washers, *H*, or with countersunk machine screws held from below by wing-nuts with washers, operating through the slots.

Set the circular saw to the required height and pass the aid over it, cutting *A*, *B* and *E*.

Remove *E* and prepare a small register block and glue it to the saw slot. *E* is re-positioned to give the required spacing between the keys, then a further cut is made.

To use, place the box in the cradle with the true edge against the register block and make a cut at each corner. The next cut is made with this first slot on the register block. Repeat the process.

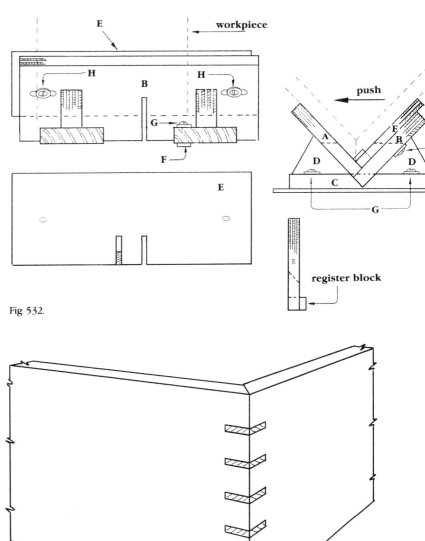

Fig 532.

If after making adjustments, the second slot in *E* becomes over-large, glue in a small block and plane flush. This will obviate 'spelching', the splintering at the end of the sawcut.

Sizes will depend upon the particular sawbench, material available and the size of work contemplated.

153

APPENDIX G

A device to construct comb (or finger) joints on the sawbench

Either screw the main block *A* to the crosscut slide or glue it to a thick block *X*, and that in turn to a bar fitting the sawbench groove. Make two slots for the screws which secure *B*. Screw the adjustable fence *B* through from behind *A*. Adjust the saw by wobble washers to give the required width of cut and set it to the height required.

Pass over the saw to give the first slot. Remove *B*, prepare a register block *C* and glue it into this slot. Replace *B*, move it sideways the thickness of the slot and temporarily secure it. Make a series of cuts on scrap pieces, adjusting *B* until a good fit is obtained over the width of the job. After adjustment, a glued-in block *D* prevents the saw from breaking out the corner of the slots.

Start with the long sides, true edge leading and pushed hard against the register block. Cut both ends of both pieces. To cut the short sides, place the first cut of a long side over the register block, push the short side hard against this and make the open-sided cut. With the open-sided cut against the register block, continue to cut as described.

To produce a mitred corner, temporarily cramp on a false face *E* which masks the register block. Where the mitre is only required on one edge, it is easier to start cutting at the other edge and stop short at the mitred edge.

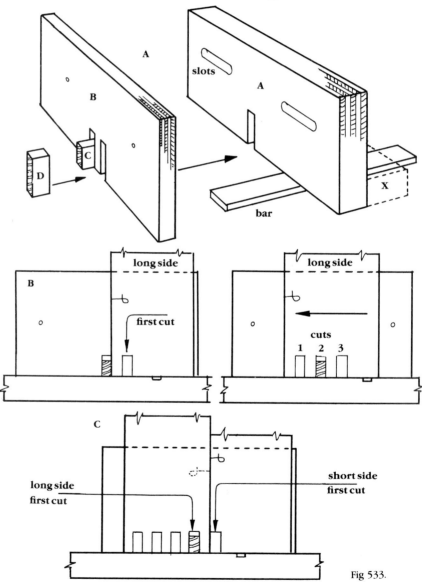

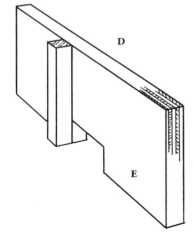

Fig 533.

APPENDIX H

Drawer slip cramps

These cramps are easily made from offcuts of any dense hardwood. The lower or fixed block is tapped to accept the screws. Use a taper tap only and work until the tip just emerges, thus ensuring an undersized hole. The screw is forced in by means of two lock-nuts. The holes in the top or moving block are drilled oversize to give a sloppy fit. A nut and wing-nut, together with two washers, complete the job. Do not neglect the washers or the jaws will quickly be chewed up.

The best fast thread to use is the 5/16in. Whitworth, but the metric M8 or American threads are equally successful. When using them, keep the jaws as parallel as possible. (See p.133).

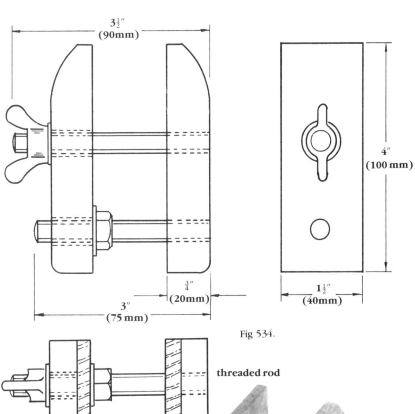

$3\frac{1}{2}''$
(90mm)

$\frac{3}{4}''$
(20mm)

$3''$
(75 mm)

$4''$
(100 mm)

$1\frac{1}{2}''$
(40mm)

Fig 534.

threaded rod

drawer slip cramp

Fig 51.

APPENDIX I

Diminishing dovetails
To divide a line into a given number of parts in steadily decreasing proportions

Draw the base line *AB*. From point *O*, draw *OC* at say 25°, *OC* being the length of the line. From *O* erect a perpendicular, *OD*.

From *O* draw *OE*, the proportions *DE* and *DO* being, say, 1:2. Project *OE*, driving in a pin along *OE* at, say, 250mm (10in.)

from *O*. Join the pin through *C* to *B*. Divide *OB* into the required number of equal parts by construction, dividers or measurement. With a rule always on the pin, connect up to these divisions to cut *OC*. These are the required decreasing proportions.

The farther out, or to the left, the pin is positioned, the less will be the diminishing; the closer the pin, the greater the diminishing.

Setting out diminishing dovetails

Repeat the basic diagram. Mark *OC* to the length of the component, and from the pin project the line to *B*. Divide up *OB* in the dovetail proportions required, making due allowance for mitred corners, sawn-off lids, etc. Project towards the pin from *OB*, cutting *OC*, giving the spacing to be applied to the job.

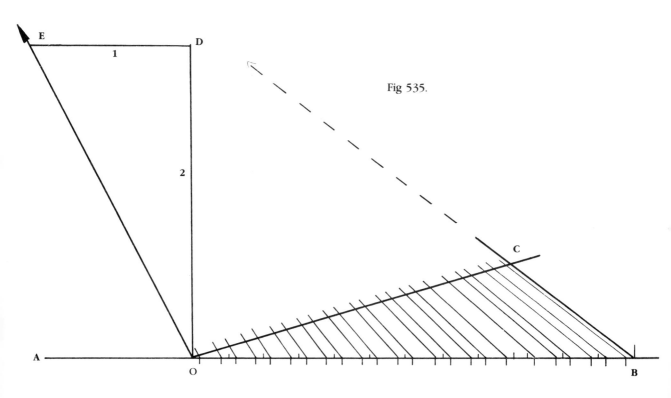

Fig 535.

BIBLIOGRAPHY

A E Bradshaw *Handmade Woodwork of the 20th Century*, J Murray, 1962.

Margery Brown, *Cane & Rush Seating*, Batsford, 1976.

Charles Hayward, *Cabinet Making for Beginners*, Evans Bros, 1949 &c.

Charles Hayward, *Tools for Woodwork*, Evans Bros, 1946 &c.

Charles Hayward, *Woodwork Joints*, Unwin Hyman, 1950 &c.

Charles Hayward, *Woodworkers' Pocketbook*, Unwin Hyman, c.1950 &c.

Ernest Joyce, *The Technique of Furniture Making*, Batsford, 1987.

Tom Petit, *Woodwork Made Simple*, W G Allen, 1977.

Patrick Spielman, *Gluing & Clamping*, Sterling USA, 1986, Blandford Press UK.

Robert Wearing, *Making Woodwork Aids & Devices*,. Sterling USA, 1985.

Robert Wearing, *Woodwork Aids & Devices*, Unwin Hyman, 1981.

MAGAZINES

Woodworker (Monthly), Argus Specialist Publications.

Practical Woodworking (Monthly), IPC Magazines.

Fine Woodworking (bi-monthly), Taunton Press USA.

INDEX

Awls   89

Backs   97
  grooved in   98
  planted   99
  rebated   98
  tongue and grooved   100
Ball catches   120
Bevel-edged chisels   89
Bits   33
  centre   33
  countersink   32
  dowelling   34, 61
  flat   34
Boring   33
Box
  cleaning up   145
  hinging   143
  joints   138
Boxes   138
Brace   33
Buttons, shrinkage   47, 75

Cabinet backs   97
  bases   123
Carcase cramp   84
Carcase
  dowelled   80
  forms   79
  glue-up   103
Cellulose lacquers   77
Centre bit   33
Chisels   39
  bevel-edged   89
Cleaning up
  insides   48
  outsides   53
Comb joint   154
Compass (or circular) plane   68
Coping saw   87
Countersink bit   32
Curves, marking   68
Cutting gauge   93
Cutting list   35

Design
  brief   35
  sketch   35
Diagonals
  correcting   50
  testing   50
Door types   106
  fitting   116
  framed construction   112
Dovetail markers   86, 93
  marking out   86
  types   84
Dovetailed carcase   84
Dovetails
  cramping bracket   89
  cutting   87
  diminishing   156
  lap   92
  machine   92
Dowelling
  aid   82
  bit   61
  carcase   80
Dowels
  grooving   62
  marker pins   61
Drawer
  bottom   128
  fitting   131
  framing   134
  joints   126
  making   126
  method   128
  slip cramps   133, 155
  slips   130
Edging   22
Edge grip   23
  jointing   59
Edge shapes   70
End grain planing   19
Escutcheons   122
Exercises, planing   20

Facing   21

Finger joint   154
Flatbit   34

Gauges
  cutting   87
  marking   26
  mortice   39
Gauging   26
Glass   145
Glues   53
Gluing up   49
Grinding   10
Grooved mitre joint   150, 151

Handles   135
Hinging
  box   143
  door   118
Honing   8

Jack plane   15
Jointing, top   59
Joints
  box   138
  carcase   80, 84, 85
  comb (or finger)   154
  door   112, 114
  grooved mitre
    by router   150
    by sawbench   151
  keyed mitre   153

Keyed mitre joint   153

Lap dovetail   92
Levelling feet   78
Lock, fitting   121

Machine dovetails   92
Markers, dovetail   86, 93
Marking gauge   26
Marking knife   29
Mirrors   145
Mitred boxes, gluing   152

158

Mortice gauge 39
Mortice and tenon
  correcting 46, 49, 50
  for table or stool 36
Morticing 41

Oil finish 76

Painting 77
Painting sticks 77
Planes
  adjustment 12
  jack 15
  scraper 63
  sharpening 8
  smoothing 53, 54
  try- 59
Planing 8
  exercises 20
  how to plane 15
Polishing
  insides 48

outsides 53
Polyurethane varnish 76
Producing to size 28

Rip tenon saw 148

Sawing 20
Sawing board 147
Scraper
  cabinet 56
  plane 63
Scratch tool 71
Screwing 32
Screws, drilling for 32
Sharpening 8
Shelf joints 95
Shelves 94
Shoulder planes 52
Shrinkage buttons 47, 75
Smoothing plane 53, 54
Spelching 19
Spokeshaves 67

Squaring 29
Strop 10

Table construction 35
Table top
  holding 68
  shapes 66
Tapers, planing 47
Tearing, cures 13
Tenon saw 20
Tenons
  correcting 46
  sawing 43
Tryplane 59
Trysquare 29
Twist bit 34

Wax polish 76
Wedges, sawing 94
Winding strips 22, 51
Working drawing 35